Stop Chasing Time; Choose Quality Time.

A practical guide that takes you from stress, disconnect and fighting the flow of life to freedom and joy!

Tanya Adams

To Victoria,

Thank you for being you & for being an amazing Reiki Teacher (among other things).

Love & Blessings
Tanya xxx.

All Rights Reserved.

Copyright © Tanya Adams

No part of this book may be reproduced or transmitted in any form or by any means, electrical or mechanical, including photocopying and recording, or by any information storage or retrieval system without permission in writing from the author.

Disclaimer:

This book is written for informational purposes only. The author has made every effort to make sure the information is complete and accurate. All attempts have been made to verify information at the time of this publication and the author does not assume any responsibility for errors, omissions, or other interpretations of the subject matter.

The publisher and author shall have neither liability nor responsibility to any person or entity with respect to any loss or damage caused or alleged to be caused directly or indirectly by this book.

Table of Contents

Acknowledgements v

Testimonials vii

Chapter 1: Introduction 1

Part I

Chapter 2: Introduction to the Seasonal Cycle and our Profound Connection with Nature 9

Chapter 3: The Seasonal Cycle and Personal Connection 23

Part II

Chapter 4: Understanding Your Chakras 65

Chapter 5: Powering up! Working with the Chakras and the Seasons 89

Part III

Chapter 6: Integrating these Practices into Everyday Life and Situations. 99

Chapter 7: Facing and Healing Difficult Anniversaries and Annual Celebrations 103

About the Author 108

Acknowledgements

Personally I can't believe that this book, as short and small as it is, even exists. Behind it lies many beautiful and insightful books from writers, healers and shamans who have kept me company and inspired with their written works at times of some, personally, very long and lonely months.

It is also the product of having danced a life between the throng of urban living and the expanse of country life; having at times flown on the wings of nature.

Most of all, having had the great gift of some beautiful people in my life including; friends, family teachers, shamans and healers.

Special thank you to, Paul, Hazel, Jan, Simon, Suneet, Phillip, Victoria, Yvonne, Samatha, Suzie, Rebecca, Naureen, Peta, Richard, Helen, Sandra, Uta, Nicola, Ken.

xxx

Testimonials

"I have worked with Tanya on a personal level and in a group setting. Tanya is by far one of the most humble and powerful healers I know. She knows her stuff and has helped me and my family immensely. She has such a kind, loving and compassionate nature making me feel very comfortable to express myself. She cleared my home a couple of years back and it made such a difference, leaving my home feeling peaceful and calm.

On a personal level she had helped me heal and grow on a spiritual level and taught me lots of tools that I now use in my spiritual practice. I would highly recommend Tanya as she works with integrity, honesty and love."

Yvonne Douglas – Spiritual Healing Coach.

***

"I had an amazing and profound ancestral healing which placed a lot of my issues that I had been facing in life in perspective.

Tanya went on to do a Past Life Regression where I found out details of some of my previous life's which helped me understand why I was drawn to my current profession. Everything just clicked into place. Thank you Tanya xx"

SG Hendon

***

I have found Tanya a very devoted and enthusiastic Shamanic Practitioner. She has helped me recognise what barriers may have been blocking me psychologically. By her example of totally honouring this work and doing it with groundedness, humility, reverence and respect, she has brought me back to reconsider 'shamanism' as a tool for our own conscious journeying.

RL London

Chapter 1
Introduction

Stress is a major cause of many chronic and serious illnesses, both physical and mental. It costs economies billions every year in lost work days and productivity, let alone the utter devastation that can occur to an individual or their family due to illness, loss of income or employment. There are thousands of programs and personal development courses available either on-line, in books or through professional coaches and therapists on how to reduce stress, all of which help to tackle this enormous and at times overwhelming "black dog" of the modern world and society.

At the age of 36 I suffered an extreme stress reaction, at the time I was living and working in London, living a busy professional life. The end result was that it took me into realms I had never dreamt of, and most of all led me to search for understanding of the causes of this type of reaction and how to heal it. One thing I quickly realised was that the way I had been living was not sustainable and had to change. I also realised that there were many deeper underlying issues that needed to be faced, understood and healed. The most unexpected result of all was that it took me into the world of alternative and holistic health and undertaking a 3 year Shamanic Apprenticeship. Shamanism is the oldest form of healing known to man, stretching back 30,000 years. The roots of most healing practices and even those of modern medicine can be traced back to these ancient practices. It is important to say that my experience of

Shamanic practice has been one of a spiritual way of life and not a religious one. Furthermore while shamanism is profoundly spiritual and works with the energy of the person or place, it is also incredibly grounded and practical. After all, the people who developed these methods lived close to nature and were probably more vulnerable on a daily basis than we are today, both to the ravages of the elements or the fierceness of the wild-beast.

A positive aspect to this picture is that it has actually now been shown in a number of academically structured and scientific studies that nature is still one of the greatest and biggest stress relievers. Some easy access references are available through The Guardian-https://www.theguardian.com/sustainable-business/nature-workshops-healing-power-nature. Studies have also been carried out at Plymouth University and the University of East Anglia. Both have conducted interesting research into the power of nature and access to greenery in increasing people's ability to heal or become less aggressive. If you wish to delve academically deeper, books such as "Forests, Trees and Human Health and Well-being: Introduction"; and "The emotional nature of qualitative research"; both by K Gilbert are useful references. I have to say I have not read these books in their entirety but have attended presentations on the material. However, these works and numerous others have shown that something as simple as a walk in a park or some time in nature reduces stress hormones, aggression and even speeds up healing more than any single other intervention. Frankly it is something that has been known by the Shamans, Yogi, Toaist Monks, Tai

Chi and Qi-Gong Masters for a very long time, perhaps just not stated in these terms.

The very diverse and huge field of Biodynamics, which is "the study of physical motion or dynamics in living systems" has been a term used for organic farming which incorporates certain astrological and spiritual principles and practices. Put simply it explores the relationship between humans and nature and often returns to the very simple but inescapable fact that we are organic beings living on an organic planet and our very being through its very nature and evolution, naturally responds and relates to organic and natural plants. Hence nature forming such a central part of our recovery and well-being programmes.

The Natural systems can be overriden in many ways through our own attitude or mind-set there are many tools and technologies which help to prevent us from becoming victim of seasonal changes or environmental threats. In fact this is something we are often encouraged to do in our modern lifestyles and busy society networks, through long working hours, '24 hour society', poor eating, fast food, and convenience living. While this is OK for a while, in the long term it has detrimental effects to our sleep and eating patterns, both of which impact profoundly on our ability to function physically as well as affecting our moods and brain functioning. Short-term we get sluggish or bad tempered; long-term it can lead to more serious health issues such as high blood pressure, obesity, heart disease, intestinal issues, toxic build up and mental disorders. Hence there is a strong for need holidays and rest periods in our schedules.

This type of fast 24 hour living, and the accompanying supportive infrastructure not only affects our health on a personal scale but it also opens up the door to global issues such as Climate Change from increased pollution, ecological damage and deforestation. In many ways it causes a domino effect where we are ravaging the very things that actually help to bring balance and well-being not just to ourselves but to the plant as a whole.

So what happens if we start to actually work with the planet? Work with the seasons? Or work with our own bodies rhythms?

There seems to be the underlying fear that suddenly kicks in at this point that we are going to be some how left behind by our competitors or colleagues, we are going to be ridiculed or become the "country bumpkin" on the block.

What if this is not the case and actually by going with the natural rhythms you actually enhance your life? What if it also could mean that your days, months and years are not just passing in one blur of meetings, schedules, appointments and targets?

What if there was a system which gave you a deeper sense of where you are and perhaps even more importantly gave you a way of constructively re-orientating yourself at times when things are not necessarily working out "as planned"?

The system in this book and the on-line teaching program connects you with a system that has been around for eons. It draws on timeless teachings from around the world and presents in a way that makes them accessible, relevant and potentially very healing for you to use through the year, it can even be applied to key projects, decisions or issues in your life. The really great part is that by working with this system, you are connecting with something that is as old as the earth and therefore is very well tried and tested.

Many diets and health programmes work on the basis of eating seasonally. There has been growing evidence, particularly through the study of bees and their feeding or nectar gathering, that by eating locally we not only get the benefits of eating the foods which are supporting our bodies during that season, but also the specific nutrients and antibodies we need to keep our bodies strong specific to the environment in which we live. Here are some other references on this subject; www.cpre.org.uk "Why you should buy and eat local food" and http://www.greenmedinfo.com/blog/raw-honey-contains-probiotic-boosts-immunity. "The Miracle of Honey" by Dr Penny Stanway. Of course this is providing we can grow our produce with minimal negative external pollutants negating their health benefits.

Our bio rhythms, sleep patterns, emotions and energy levels are affected to some degree by the weather and the season that we are living in. Each season has many associations, gestures and symbolism. When we tune into these and understand what they mean for us, we can open up a far more insightful connection with our environment and ourselves and be able to change how we approach our tasks, jobs, family and community. They may even manifest in our dreams.

If you do a lot of travel, or your lifestyle requires you to have a long or flexible schedule, or involves shift work your daily life is likely to be quite shifted from the natural daily rhythms. However the exercises and systems in this book are very relevant. In some ways perhaps they are even more important, as the disconnect from these natural rhythms are potentially even greater; being able to consciously reconnect will help you maintain balance.

In Part I of this book I will take you through the year, its seasons, and the symbolism and gesture of each one. The associations in terms of emotions and actions of that season and the deeper connection that we still hold with these times, including what it potentially teaches us and what is most helpful to consider are outlined.

Please note the format of the year's cycle within this book is based on the Northern Hemisphere, so if you are living in the southern hemisphere, please reverse the patterns and for those that live around the equator, the fluctuations are less extreme, however, you will no doubt find certain patterns in the descriptions, which you can relate to with your own seasons.

While following the year in this way can be considered "Pagan" and the insights and symbolism is drawn from many of these ancient and indigenous teachings, it is worth considering that also these points of the year are also marked out in the Christian and other religious calendars. The material in this book and the on-line program seeks to bring personal insight and connection to the natural world and rhythms only. It is founded solely within the bounds of personal development and spiritual insight. All of these exercises and practices are based on ancient systems, however they are offered in a way that is totally about enabling you to develop your own connection to nature and your energy system without religious bias and you are free to bring into your own private process your own belief practices if you wish.

In developing your own expression of these practices or exercises, please be mindful of the true time of the year and the seasonal expression you are living in at that time. Otherwise you are simply once again overiding a natural and profound rhythm and potentially missing a vital connection to your own emotional and physical need.

Part II of the book is presented in seven sections which works through the Chakra system; going into more detail of what this system is, the different associations, and how they play a key role in your life. A series of exercises and recommendations on how to work with these at certain times during the seasonal cycle are included at the end of this section. This draws it into a single program that flows with the ebb and flow of the year, enabling times of increased action and strength and times for pause, reflection and renewal.

The Chakra exercises can be practiced at any time; the invitation is to work with them particularly during times where the season is shifting to strengthen, realign and align for the next season.

Part III, the final part of the book brings together the year cycle and the chakra work and expands on how this system can be applied to other life activities or programmes in your life and activities which do not necessarily track the year because their duration is either shorter or even longer than the cycle of one year. It also includes a section on coping with, facing and healing difficult anniversaries.

It is recommended that you read through this book and become familiar with the exercises and associations. You can begin the individual Chakra Exercises as soon as you wish. To get the most out of the material in this book and the on-line programme it is recommended that you work with the Season Practices at the time of the season. When you feel you are familiar with the material and the exercises apply the guidelines and exercises contained in Part III to as many things in your life as you wish.

PART I

Chapter 2
Introduction to the Seasonal Cycle and our Profound Connection with Nature

"Everything Has Its Time
To everything there is a season,
A time for every purpose under heaven:"
Ecclesiastes 3

In everyday modern life, we have a tendency of thinking about time and our daily existence as linear. We are born, we grow up, we become adults perhaps parents and grandparents, watch our children enter the same process and then finally die.

The day starts, we have breakfast, we go to work, or school or whatever our daily schedule is; at some point things come to a close at night and we go to sleep. If you are working a night shift, the connection with natural cycles of day light is significantly disrupted. The start and end get more blurred since your life tends to totally revolve around the shift of your work schedule; when it starts and finishes and the organising of your activities, even your sleep within the 24 hours. However, there is still a revolving and evolving pattern.

If we start a course or project, we set our goals, or have certain targets to meet and there is always a programme of the steps to take to get to the end and there is a sense that the goals or deliverables are either met or not. Pass or fail, good or bad.

While this dualistic and linear element in our lives and daily schedule there is actually another pattern that is far older and far bigger and far more holding and it is going on all around us. Literally A Round Us……

We are on a globe, a beautiful blue and green globe, that is spinning and turning. Going round and round. Which of course means we get day and night and light all around the planet. The Earth so beautifully tilts on its access at 23.5 degrees to the sun. This tilt combined with the fact it then, while spinning, travels around the sun results in the seasonal fluctuations. The spinning and seasonal fluctuations provide a self-sustaining system which all plants, animals and even humans respond to. Nature in itself, or herself, just like our bodies, seek an overall state of homeostasis. This is the body's natural ability to maintain a constant temperature (within a small range) and life providing rhythms such as blood flow, heartbeat, breath. In the wider environment nature and ecology constantly shows us how important balance is, how delicate that balance can be and how when we look deep enough we find that there is an incredible web of inter-dependence between species and incredible fluctuations brought by the seasons that drive, steer and dictate that ecological balance.

In many ways in the interests of survival and success humans have sought to understand the senses and control them. Seeking control of the senses, while it has led to some profound discoveries and advances has equally led to incredible devastation, loss and imbalances. Our modern life, in many ways and thanks to all of these advances and new technology more often than not takes us away from the direct impact of nature and insulates us from much of the rawness of nature, such as extreme wet, cold or heat conditions. While this clearly leads to a more comfortable life in many ways, there is a price and not all of it is about deforestation and chemical toxicity. There is a deeper connection that we begin to lose and it can have a potentially profound impact on our own instinctive insight and stress levels.

For many years I worked in the development industry and in the corporate world, working to programmes, engaging project management tools, very much aware of the start – finish, deliver or fail time line. When I came out of that world I started to work far more closely with the natural cycle of the year. I first learnt about diet and the energetic movement through year, our bodies and our emotional states by studying and experiencing the ancient system of the Chinese Five Elements. Later on I was worked more with the seasons and the Celtic 8 Seasonal Celebrations and 4 Elements or 7 Directions, (something I had already been aware of as a very young adult) in many ways the indigenous system to the British Isles. As I worked with these systems and started to apply them more and more into my own life, it became so clear how one thing leads to another and how we are not really living a linear existence but one that is actually tracking and is a part of this greater constant cycle. In fact life is far more cyclical than linear.

The funny part was that just as I felt the relief of realising this, freed from "this is The End", "pass or fail", "I didn't fall off the edge of the earth"; I also felt a back wash fear of; "oh my goodness I'm just going around and around in this endless circle!". Then came the next revelation; we actually have the fantastic opportunity to walk a spiral. The spiral is one of the oldest symbols that appears in many indigenous cultures, depicting life, even the cycle of life, death and rebirth. Suddenly at this point I could let go of the very fixed, dualistic view which was filled with stress and with relief allow in something that is part of a much bigger, older, wiser and more expansive system.

Huge, easy breath was possible for me at this point. It was also at this point I decided to really embrace the seasons and learn far more about the traditional ways by which they were celebrated and the symbolism or gestures that go with them. Clearly much of this came from times when we all lived far closer to the land and to nature and our very existence depended on understanding those patterns. A wonderful source of information and inspiration for this came from the work of Glennie Kindred, writer and speaker. For most of us, who do not work directly with agriculture or live a subsistence lifestyle, the fluctuations of the seasons now pass us by and are often little more than an irritation or at times a rare dramatic inconvenience for example when the weather seems to get in our way after a heavy snow shower. Or, more seriously, bursts into our lives if devastation to our homes and communities has been caused by severe weather conditions, such as flooding.

So why and how are the seasons important for us now, today?

They still teach us of the stages within just about everything we do or create. They teach about the stages in our lives, they also offer the regular invitation to take stock, to renew, to check in with where we are so we can continue to the next stage, in whatever we are doing. The best thing is, is that we have this great big thing called the sun and day light to help us remember where we are and to aid our connection to these rhythms. Plus to do it you do not have to change your home, your job, your diet or your belief systems. However, you may find as you become more conscious of these rhythms and their associations, in time you might choose to make changes in your own routine. That's actually OK because it simply means you are allowing yourself to hear yourself and to make the changes you want to, or need to make. Obviously with one word of caution, please do exercise some sense if and when making big changes!

By following this rhythm, it also means that if you "failed" the first time, you get another chance, this is what the spiral shows us. It gives us lots of opportunities to learn and reshape where we are going and it means that however slim your "harvest" is, there's always a way of learning and doing things differently, renewing your motivation, while tempered with wisdom. There's a chance to release old ties or what no longer serves, to make space for the totally new. It also shows up what's overloaded, overstrained and is not working for you or your loved one's highest good. If you doubt this cycle, just remember the Earth has been doing this for a very, very, long time! We would not be here without it.

So just to be clear – there are four major solar stage points in the year. The two solstices (mid-summer and mid-winter) longest and shortest days and two equinoxes (spring and autumn) when the day light to night is equal. This has an effect on our plants and animals signalling to them times of great growth, abundance and times of receding and lack. We have for quite some time now fallen into a mind-set that says constant growth is good and anything receding is bad. In actual fact it creates balance otherwise it creates a state of excess. As anyone who has eaten too much fat, sugar, alcohol or undertaken an activity for too long can testify any excess is simply not healthy.

Our bodies react to the amount of light we receive and the quality of that light, whether it is from electric sources, computers or the sunshine. It has profound effects on our sleep patterns, vitamin and mineral levels. For any life form you need light and water. I remember visiting a cave in the Peak District and the guide pointed her torch up to the ceiling of the cavern, and among the rock formations, also pointed out a small area of moss. She said it was the first time moss was growing in this cavern and it was all because at that point water was permeating and they had erected a light which happened to shine onto this part of the rocks. Something as simple as that had introduced a new ecology into the cave.

An amazing part of studying the seasonal cycle is that we also learn that just because something slows or goes inwards, it is not necessarily a bad thing or something to be feared. Actually it is potentially and profoundly about insight and renewal.

It is not for nothing that we are encouraged to do a body cleanse in the spring as our bodies are waking up for the more active time of the year, or we are advised to take on more nutrients in autumn when the weather is getting cooler and our bodies need to be stocked up for winter. In the Chinese 5 Element system there are two very distinct 'Chi' that run through the year, these are the yin kidney chi and the yang liver chi. Essentially the yang liver chi becomes very active and is more dominant during the spring and summer months of the year, while the yin kidney chi becomes more dominant during the autumn and winter months. This is reflecting the pattern of up and outward during half of the year, while the other part is more in and downward. Neither is favoured beyond the other or seen as more important than the other, it is simply the key energy flows within the whole and a self-sustaining and balancing system.

By being aware even superficially, of these two profound energy movements and the nature of the chi, they can be supported better and rather than fight them, adapt to work with them, allowing our systems the nurture and rest or exercise they need to function well. Equally it helps us understand our moods or inner desires and rather than fight these to work with them so they become insightful and constructive experiences rather than something to be feared or ignored.

When we fear or ignore we are simply blocking what is already there and, rather than it diminishing, it often means it either starts to grow or define us rather than nurture and teach us.

There are four further stage posts through the years which are known in the Celtic tradition as the Cross-Quarters. These are the intervening, mid points between the four Solar stage points already mentioned. To me they often feel almost more lunar or feminine, as they are not so defined by the Sun's apex. They really are the subtle marker points of when a season begins or ends, while the 4 solar points mark the apex of summer, winter, or turning point of spring and autumn. The Cross-Quarters mark the very early stirrings of spring in February; the explosion of spring into summer in May; the start of the Harvesting in early August; and the very profound time of the year, that is the end of the harvest and the final slip into winter at Hallow'een, or All Hallows Day.

The next chapter will take you around the wheel of the year along with the associations and gesture for the year and its seasons. It includes exercises and practices you can use to connect with these and what to be aware of at a particular time to make it relevant to you and support you in your own personal life. First though, it would be good to do a short exercise to see how you personally relate to the seasons to help you to find out what they mean for you.

Meditation with the Seasons.

Do this in a space where you feel comfortable, safe and will not be disturbed. If you already have a place where you do your daily meditation then try this next time you are spending some time there. If you don't regularly meditate then find your most comfortable place in your space. You can make it as special as you like by lighting a candle(s), burning some oils, placing some flowers on a table. You may want to put some calming music on softly.

Read through the meditation below a few times before trying it. You may find just sitting and breathing gently in the space you have created a great way to become familiar with the process of centring and de-stressing. When you are comfortable at doing this process continue with the exercise. Alternatively, the meditation is contained in the On-line Free Teaching Segment, which accompanies this book.

As with all meditations, take some time to calm your breathing, to sense your body, centre and enjoy feeling held by your chair, cushions or if you're on the floor, simply being in contact with the earth beneath you. Sense around your body, breathing out any tensions and being conscious of the breath as almost an internal massage within your body bringing you new energy with every breath. You can visualise any tensions or unhelpful thoughts or emotions dropping away to the ground, where it is composted and transmuted to light or nothingness.

When you feel centred and your breath is easy and deepened, take your attention to your lower abdomen or the Dan Tien (a term for this power area of the body, familiar to those who practice TaiChi or QiGong) and allow yourself to be aware of energy building in this area with each breath. Then visualise yourself walking on a country path. Be focused on the walk and the grasses and flowers around you. You come to a small gate, allow yourself to pass through and into a meadow. Here in the middle of the meadow is growing a very large and old tree. Approach this tree and allow yourself to connect with it, become familiar with it and find yourself a comfortable place to sit. Know that you are held and safe.

Allow yourself to become one with this tree. Then notice the fresh green leaves on this tree and realise that it is spring. Really tune in with this vibrant and upward movement of spring. See what birds, animals or plants come to you.

After a while become aware of the weather becoming warmer and the leaves becoming bigger as it now shifts to the fullness of summer. Again see what wildlife, items or emotions and associations come forward. Then after a while become aware of the leaves on this mighty tree turning to Autumn. Don't worry about the coolness as you have everything at the tree that you need, so if you need a rug about you allow yourself to put one on. Again just see which wildlife, items or associations and emotions come to the forefront. Be assured that you are with this mighty tree, nothing bad can happen to you and you are only observing. Then as the days cool become aware of the descent of winter around you. What does it feel like? Which wildlife, items, associations or emotions come to the forefront. Again this is just about observing. After a short while become aware of the day warming again and the spring returning. When you are ready give your thanks to the mighty and ancient tree and allow yourself to return across the meadow and through the small gate onto the country path. Return along the country path and then become very aware of your breath in your body. Do move your body, your hands, feet, give a little stretch if you wish and make sure you are fully back in the room that you are physically sat in.

Make some notes of what has come up for you about each season. Please remember these are your own observations and associations with the seasons. Every season is simply following its course and has its own purpose and gesture. The associations you have with them are very much about your own emotional attachments to each one. If they are favourable and positive, you know this is a season that you flourish in. If there are associations which are more difficult where you felt uncomfortable, it is a strong indication that there is something in the gesture of this season that has a lesson or meaning for you. Understanding this more will help you shift from being drained in this season to being empowered.

With this kind of meditation or work, you are entering the world of symbolism and it is worth looking into the traditional teaching and medicines of the plants, animals or items that appeared for you during the meditation. Even more important note your own emotion, as this is coming from deep within you.

If you had very few associations, or you couldn't focus that's OK, it just takes practice and this could just be because it is new and you've not really connected in this way before. As you work through the seasons and the practical exercises within this book, you may find it gets easier.

We are actually going start our journey around the year at the Autumn Equinox. The reasons for this will become clearer when going on to work with the chakras. However it is a point in the year where many things have either completed and ended while others are just beginning. It's often a point in the year where we are returning from holiday, refreshed from the summer with exams and other tests behind us ready to start a new project, school year or gather in for the winter. It is as much about releasing as it is about starting.

Introduction to the Seasonal Cycle and our Profound Connection with Nature

THE SEASONAL WHEEL

For reflective interpretation and illustrative purposes only.

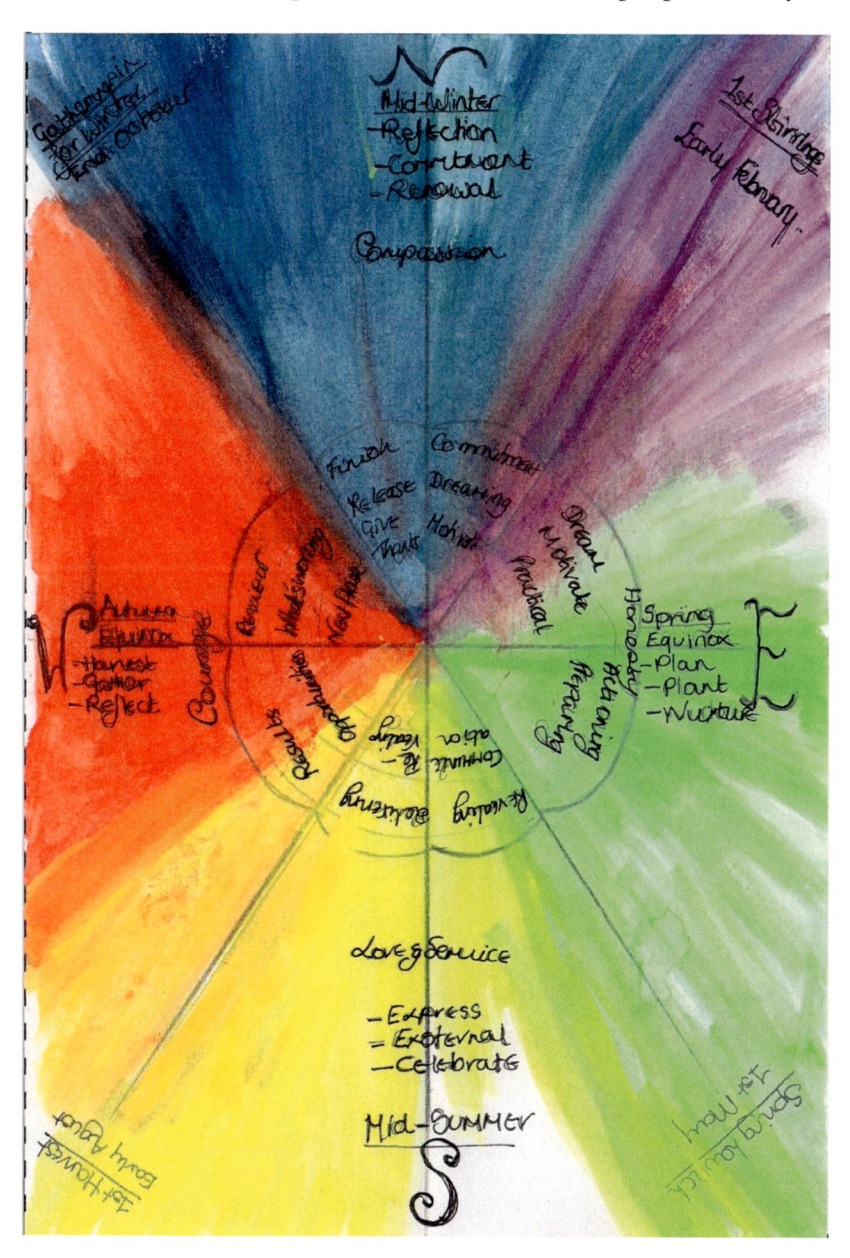

Chapter 3
The Seasonal Cycle and Personal Connection

"Nature is our greatest teacher"

- Edna Walling

This chapter works through each seasonal celebration, the associations provided in three sections, i.e. Physical, Practical and Spiritual. You are invited to embrace all of the aspects that are included in these sections. If you only have time for one or two that's OK as you can always address a different aspect next time!

Autumn Equinox - A time of Harvest and Courage.

At this time of the year the day and the night are of equal length. It marks the end of the summer harvest time and it is still abundant with late fruits. It is the turning point of the year from the fullness of summer to the Autumn colours. It falls on 21 or 22nd September (or March in Southern Hemisphere). Some find this time of year holding a sense of depression as it marks the time of things drawing in and "ending". Yet here is the harvest and the time to celebrate and often the weather is very beautiful as nature adorns her greatest colours of the year-greens, reds, oranges and golds.

The gesture of this time of year is really about Balance, Gathering, Harvesting, Review and Completion.

- **Physical** – the harvest is coming home, it's a great time to get bottling and preserving. This is a key time to stock up on your vitamins and minerals before the winter sets in. It is interesting to note that this a time when (certainly in the Northern Hemisphere) berries such as blackberries, elderberries, apples and rose hips are all prevalent and are all packed with vitamins and immune boosters. Eaten fresh they can help boost you, preserved of course means you can use them through the winter period. There are many suppliers of natural health products who offer syrups and food supplements made from these natural ingredients. If you do want to take advantage of these, please try to source ones which are ethically produced and are as near to the natural product as possible. The impact may otherwise be diminished through poor production and additives.

- **Practical** – It is time to review what you have done and what you are doing. It is a time for starting the decent into winter, as the days get shorter and cooler and we find ourselves less likely to want to go out and about and perhaps even becoming slightly less active. So it is a time to junk the stuff that has come to an end or its season has passed. Furthermore, certainly in the northern hemisphere it's a time when the new academic year starts or is a return from the summer break and actually new activities are about to take priority. It is important to make space for these. Autumn is also the season associated with conferences and shows – these all need their space whether attending as a delegate or actually taking part through running a stand or undertaking a talk or workshop. It is about embracing a shift in mode.

With this in mind the period around the Autumn Equinox is a great time to have a sort through. Balance up what is finished, what is not working and bag it, box it or clear it out. Check what is about to start, what is working for you and is on-going and actually might need its own space or a renewed space. Get ready for the next season. For the gardeners among you this will no doubt be second nature, the invitation is to extend it beyond your garden. Just do what is needed, you don't need to do every inch of the house!

- **Emotional and Spiritual** – At Equinox itself it is worth tuning into the feeling that this time evokes for you. Really tune into energy of the day and night being of equal length. Sometimes we can become so obsessed with the fact the days are getting shorter and winter is coming, that we miss it is actually a time of great balance.

Around this time, take some walks in nature, which can be even in your town park, if you live in an urban area. Just become very conscious of the colours of the trees, at this time of fruit and harvest. Allow yourself to revel in the colours. The invitation is to spend some time with a tree that calls to you and really tune into the colours and its vibrancy and give thanks for the fullness that it has given throughout the summer, whether it's shade or fruits. Take some time to reflect on what you have achieved this year. Consider how you have spent your time. What is your harvest? Be kind and honest with yourself. It does take courage to reflect in this way. Allow yourself to feel warm about what you have achieved or helped to manifest. If there are things that you have failed to do, or that have not gone well, take honest stock about why this is. This is NOT about blame. There might be a number of reasons; you didn't do the work, you didn't make sure you had enough time. Or perhaps others blocked you from achieving your goal. It's important to understand this from a compassionate place. They might have had your best interests at heart, even if this might seem or even be mis-placed. Or you might realise that they are people that are simply blocking you from achieving something that is very important to you. If it is something that you wish to continue with and continue to develop, now might be a time that you focus on attracting the people that will help you and gently letting those that have blocked you step aside.

If it is something that no longer serves you and you no longer wish to pursue, allow it to fall away out of your life just like the falling autumn leaves. Over the next few weeks as Autumn sets in, make sure you finish up or close whatever it is down. Even throw out stuff that was associated with that activity if need be. While meditating with your tree, you can even visualise it being taken down deep into the earth with each leaf that falls through the autumn.

If it is something that is that important to you and is overall in yours or others best interests trust that eventually it will happen. You will meet the right people, those that care for you will either step aside or even shift to helping you. Sometimes things get blocked because we are approaching them in the wrong way or we are not listening well enough to the one's we love. It is worth taking some time to feel where these sit with you. This includes how it feels in your body as you recall them. From this you will get a good sense about who or what supports you in achieving this goal or activity or new habit, and who does not. Choose your allies. Winter is also a good time to take a break from things, so perhaps it needs to simply "sleep" for the winter allow yourself to come back to it fresh in the spring time. If this is the case, put it consciously aside and wait to review it in the spring. Again it's often good to follow up these insights physically. This can be done by clutter clearing at home, or filing stuff away symbolically.

For example, if you have found that you didn't do very well on a course and you decide it is not the right time to restart the course, make the decision to review in the spring. Gather up your notes and books from the course and put them on a shelf that does not always catch your attention. However, don't stick them in the loft because you actually do want to review it in the Spring. Identify if there is something you need to do to help do better next time. Perhaps there is a short course that will help you with an area that you were struggling with.

If you always hung out with people from your old course, be clear within yourself about those who were or are your true friends and stay in touch. It will help you focussed to return to do the work. However, do not feel obliged to "hang out with the old crowd" as this may perhaps just be painful reminder of your "failure" and actually become counter productive. Make it clear to anyone who is simply pushing you as to why you have made this choice. If they don't or can't accept your reasons after telling them three times in a clear and constructive way, do not continue to discuss the topic with them.

If you still feel attached to the failure as opposed to the start of a 'new chapter' – mark up in your diary when you are going to revisit this topic or issue. You can undertake your own small ceremony by burning any unneeded materials from the course as a release from this "unsuccessful" experience.

Interestingly through the autumn there are many foods where the seeds are actually contained in them. When we gather them we are also gathering the seeds for the next crop and harvest. In many ways the process I've just outlined is about discarding what is done with and gathering your own seeds ready for planting. This analogy may help to remind you that from everything we do there are seeds and sometimes things have to go underground to allow them to germinate. Finally focus on the space you have created in your life, which can now be put to constructive use instead of something that has been draining you. You can use this time to build your strength, motivation and even knowledge base so that if and when you return to it you are stronger and wiser.

This is a simple example, however the principals can be applied to many other activities or events in our lives. Autumn is a great time to take stock, gather in and to shed that which no longer serves us.

The natural tree energy that is particularly present at this time is Apple. Apples are packed with nutrients, they have very mystical and spiritual associations and they show us also that things that fruit late can be the most nutritious and within them hold the seeds for the next, not just the harvest but seeds for an orchard. It is worth looking at what is in your life that reminds you of the good apples, the bad apples and those that you wish to sow!

Gathering in For Winter - Hallow'een or Samhuin or All Hallows.

This is a very special time of year and one that many of you will know mainly for the party frolics and no doubt associate with ghosts and ghouls. It does of course fall at the end of October.

Traditionally this was a time when all the cattle were brought down from the high hills into stabling and shelter. The harvest was long gathered in and really it was about making sure that the gathered harvest and stabled cattle would make it through the winter. In the Celtic year this was actually the New Year. This was the time to say good bye to the old and prepare for the new. The preparations, though, were done for the winter sleep and survival. There would be a huge festival and for 3 days between Samhuin or Hallow'een and 3rd of November the normal rules would break down. People could party and even new intimate partnerships were formed.

Spiritually this is a time when, with the darkening of the days, the vale between the worlds grows very thin, and contact with the other side became easy. Hence it became known as the time for ghosts and ghouls. However, the old celebrations were far more about evoking and honouring the Ancestors; for we would not be here without them and one day we will be one!

It is the seasonal time of going within and where the inward journey of nature and our own beings really is announced. With the darkening nights there is a profound shift in our own body rhythms and our pituitary glands actually respond to this shift in day light, or the lack of light. They become more active and through this activation sensitivity can increase. Hence the darkness allows us to connect better with our inner-self. Sometimes people find this challenging and even frightening. This in a society that tends to places a lot of emphasis on the external appearance and external world, in many ways can feel like an unchartered journey. So here are some pointers to help you connect with this very powerful time of year in a way that takes you beyond the 'trick or treating' and the rubber masked ghouls, to the essence and magical soul of this time.

- **Physical** – The nights are drawing in the days are shorter and the weather is cooler. It is the last part of autumn where the final leaves fall to the ground and it begins to be more winter than autumn. Now is an important time to eat wholesome and good food and funnily enough it is a time that is rich with the root vegetable. Of course pumpkins are not just for carving, they make great soups, casseroles and bakes. Just as our ancestors did, it is a great time to gather in and make the most of the home comforts. Feather your nest as it were, for winter. Nurturing our bodies in this way also helps us deal far better with any underlying issues we may have with regards cold weather, and darkness as well as supporting our immunity.

- **Practical** – In the Chinese five elements the element of this time is Metal. It is all about contracting, clarity and the classic metal day is the dry, clear autumn day. The energy is very much about completing and finishing off. This can sit a little uncomfortably in someways with the academic year which has only just got going. However, in recognising the presence of this energy you can work with it rather than fear it. For anything that is nearing completion or for which it is time to be finished, aim complete this by Hallow'een. This also has a great effect of leaving you clear for the Christmas Season (if you live in the northern hemisphere) which as we know is an incredibly busy time.

The parties that are associated with this time are a great way to remind us of the kind of warmth that we ourselves can generate with our loved ones.

- **Emotional and Spiritual** – The energy at this time of year does open us up to the darkness and may go beyond the darkness which brings in all the associations with ghosts and the after life. In the Celtic Four Element system this is a time which is associated with Water which holds the properties of seer-ship, emotion, the dreamtime and the otherworlds. A huge part of the celebrations were, and still are today, about honouring and remembering our ancestors and giving thanks. Where the relationships were difficult or the people themselves when they walked this earth were troublesome, clearly this can be more challenging. If we hold on to the hurt, the hate and fear then we do become haunted whether emotionally or literally. When we can release the hurt compassionately and turn the hate to a place of forgiveness and learning, it brings an energy release that is healing for those who are still walking on this earth and it sends out an energy ripple into the universe that brings healing on many levels.

The energy of this time is incredibly powerful for connecting with deep insight and release. Once again, it is about having the courage to look within.

The invitation at this time of year is to connect with the spirit of completing, giving thanks to those that have gone before and to release that which no longer serves.

All the exercises below need to be undertaken in a place where you feel you are held, where it is safe, and ideally if you have a space in your own place which you already use for daily meditation or practice.

If you don't, then make sure you set up a space for the purposes of these exercises. It needs to be a place where you feel safe, where you won't be disturbed and where you can safely bring in items such as candles, crystals, incense and soft music with the sole intention of creating a space which has a warm and caring environment. When we release or get in touch with those things that are deeper or perhaps more emotional it is unwise to do so in a space where we already feel unsettled. You can ask for angelic protection and guidance throughout the time you create and hold your own ceremony; I highly recommend this, however, it is your choice. It is also important at the end of your meditation time or personal ceremony that you clear away items that associated with the heavier parts of the ceremony, such as any personal writing, used tissues, burnt incense or candle left overs, disposing and discarding them in a responsible manner. Ensure you consciously disconnect from the energy that they represent. Cleanse any items that you may wish to keep in your space such as crystals. It is important, particularly if the session has been bringing up lots of difficult memories or emotions, to open the windows, shake out any cushions or blankets you've been using, burn some incense (sage, lavender, sandlewood), or use some angelic crystal room sprays, rattles, drums or singing bells/bowls to cleanse the space at the end of the ceremony. You don't want to later on walk back into the energy of a finished ceremony!

Sacred Space making and Ceremony holding is a subject all of its own, "Space Cleansing: how to energize your home using ancient rituals to purify and harmonize your living space" by Stella Martin is a good guide. However, these pointers can help you create your own space and ceremony on a very simple level. If you feel you need more guidance or issues are larger than you can deal with on your own, seek appropriate advice.

Once your space is set up spend some moments centring and breathing easily. Ground yourself by becoming aware of your body and the ground, cushions or seat beneath you. Visualise your own roots from your feet going down deep into the earth connecting with her crystalline waters and deeper down to her fiery centre. Become aware of energy branches reaching up above you and connecting with the sky and the stars above. Allow this light to fill your being. Take your attention to your lower abdomen or Dan Tien and just feel what is sitting there. There may be things that you wish to create that you have either undertaken this year or have laid dormant. Allow these to come to surface. Allow yourself to be content and pleased with those things you have completed this year or are going successfully. Allow that internal smile to grow. Take some time looking and feeling into those things that bubble up that are not completed or are present in your life and do not bring you joy. They might be activities, behaviours, habits or destructive beliefs. Feel into which ones do not serve you going forwards and you are basically done with. Write these down on a piece of paper.

Spend some time giving thanks for all you do have in your world and your life. Take some time to feel into your own ancestral lines, your mother's side and your father's side. Feel what the emotions are that you have around these family lines. For those that feel warm, allow yourself to reflect on these people or just the warmth and give love and thanks. For those that feel cool or darker, ask for healing for you, for them and for the lineage. If there are areas which contain bad or destructive relationships, ask again for healing and forgiveness. You can visualise a purple light encompassing them, you and any energetic link between you and them. If you feel that this person whoever they are, do not belong in your personal space, ask for this link or chord to be unhooked. Visualise light coming to you, going to them and filling any gap that is created through this boundary creation. If you do not wish their relationship in your life any longer write this down on the paper.

Feel into where your energy boundaries sit and if anyone is linking into this in a way that is not loving or is in any way draining. Visualise and unhook these gently until you become aware of a light bubble all around you. Always when unhooking do it with love and with the intention that healing is received by all parties. It is the most healing route otherwise in many ways all you do is set yourself up for an "energy mudslinging contest". This does not serve anyone and least of all – YOU!

Become aware of your body, the warmth that now surrounds you and the space that you are in. Finally, carefully burn the piece of paper on which you have written all those things that no longer serve you or you no longer wish to be in your life. Burn it with the intention that, as you release them they are transmuted and space is made to bring healing and insight into your life. You may want to burn incense or an oil at the same time. Sage, Frankincense, Lavender, Cedarwood or Cinnamon are all good for this.

As this is a time and an exercise which is likely to bring up deep emotion or issues, if you find this happens then please don't just sit on it, seek further appropriate assistance and advice if need be.

The tree that is most associated with this time of year is the Yew. The Yew is an incredible tree, it is evergreen and poisonous; however, Taxol, a chemical which comes from the Yew, is actually used in some treatments of cancer. The Yew tree is the classic tree of graveyards. The tree gesture is actually about the continuous life cycle emphasised by its evergreen properties and the fact that it grows by 'hollowing' where new trees grow from its spreading branches and roots. It is also known as the 'God Tree'.

If you can do nothing else at Hallow'een or Samhuin, it is worth going for a walk, allow yourself to observe and connect through meditation with your own local Yew trees. You will at some level, tune into the spirit of this time of year, and thereby receive your own insight and guidance.

Mid-Winter and the Winter Solstice

This is the apex of the dark days, and the shortest day of the year, falling on 21/22nd December. Everything will have gone to ground, although often the actual real chill and test of winter endurance is still to come. It is called the Solstice, because in terms of the trajectory of the solar cycle, the sun actually takes a pause on this day as the cycle shifts from one of contraction to one of expansion. The good news is that we have hit the end of the darkening, and from here on for the next six months it is all about things once again lightening and eventually warming.

This time teaches about the renewal process, that it does take time. It is worth considering that the season gesture has been one of contraction and going to ground for quite some time, having been most strongly felt from the time of the Autumn Equinox. Even though the days will now start to lengthen it will take some time for things to re-emerge from the ground. This period is not wasted, nor is it just a time of endurance. Nature shows us every year that actually there needs to be a time of going inward and going to ground, so that everything gets a rest and during this slumber much is happening below ground. I'll explore this more in the next section about the first stirrings of spring. Mid-Winter is really about connecting with this point of deep inward movement and completion. This becomes the transition from something ending to a new start.

The Chinese Element for this time is Water which is about the depths, the abyss and the emotion, while the Celtic Element is Earth. Interestingly, in the Chinese system, Earth controls or holds water. For me what this combined gesture really shows is how much this time of year, brings stillness and how renewal comes from these depths of the stillness. Clearly a time for us too, to be still, to hear our inner wisdom and release our emotions or heal and let go of what might have been stored up.

This can only be done in the holding presence of great compassion, which is an emotion synonymous with the nurturing element of earth. So rather than these two systems being at odds, they echo the same language for gesture of winter.

The gesture of this time is about Compassion, Reflection, Rejuvenation, and Commitment and Renewal

In the northern hemisphere mid-winter is shortly before the New Year and of course this is always a time for New Year's resolutions. Well actually the energy of the year is such that it is not a great time to start and action a new programme, however, it is an excellent time to make the commitment and make ready for a new programme or regime.

- **Practical** – As the year or the inward cycle is completing, now from an almost uninvolved place, from a place of pure observation, is a great time to just reflect on how the year really has been for you. Make sure that it is well tempered between the "good and the bad" and if it has been a truly "bad" year, look for the lessons in this and be grateful that you have made it through. Gratitude in the face of adversity can be a really hard thing to take on, however, it is a saviour in many ways, as it shifts us from a place of despondency and victim to place of presence and action. It warms us within and brings the heartiness back into us that we need to move forward to face the next chapter.

In the northern hemisphere it is of course coming up to Christmas, a busy time with the family and sometimes we get jettisoned from our normal daily life to suddenly facing relatives who perhaps we have not seen for a long time or don't have much in common with, or simply with whom we don't get on with. However, what this season does do is get us in touch with our roots. Where we come from, what made us who we are. When we can look at it from this perspective we can be grateful in terms of how we have evolved and no matter how much we might feel we are being squashed back into a "box" that people have classified us as being in, we can be assured it is not reality. It is also worth remembering that family members, however annoying they might be, also have the habit of testing out how real our evolution actually is. The best tonic is a good dose of humour.

If there is genuine abusive or destructive behaviour, then choose who you want to spend Christmas with. Most importantly do it from a place of loving honesty and not revenge.

- **Physical** – This is the depth of winter and our bodies need good nurturing food, so be mindful of this. We also have a tendency to over eat and over indulge at this time. It is fine to have a splurge, in fact in many ways it is healthy and good for our psychie. However, too much is too much. If you do over indulge, make sure you replenish your body with the vital nutrients or eat a bit lighter for a few days. I remember years ago as a young professional, and my first Christmas in the "big smoke"; I had so many parties and late nights that towards Christmas I literally wasn't sure if I was going to make it through. I survived and then, luckily, I had some days off and just slept. Some friends criticised me for this and even suggested there was something wrong with me. Actually it was the best thing I could have done so that I was ready and replenished for the next part of winter.

It is worth noting here that the gesture of Water in the Chinese elements is lying down and for Earth in the Celtic system it is hibernation or the cave, the stillness. So when we go against this, it is hardly surprising that we end up with more colds and sickness in the winter time, because we are in many ways over-riding and potentially damaging our own body's rhythms.

- **Emotional and Spiritual** – This is a time for reflection on what has been and your journey through the year, and as the things that hopefully you completed or released in the Autumn period. Allow yourself to become conscious of these once again and take note of how things have been and what kind of space has been created for you either physically or emotionally in your life by the finishing or release.

If you have had a tough year, or certain things have been very draining for you, make sure you take some time over the Solstice, to connect with the sun at this 'stand still'. This can be through meditation, a walk or something very nurturing like a spa day or massage. This will give your body and emotions a chance to be nurtured to express themselves and to heal. Sometimes we keep going because we are afraid that if we stop we will connect with negative emotions. Actually it is healthy to cry and if we don't take that time to allow ourselves to express such deeper emotions then it's like an emotional bin that never gets emptied. Nurturing ourselves also sends the good message to our senses on all levels that although "bad" or "tough" things happen we are capable of generating the reverse, we have the capacity to care for ourselves. This can be incredibly empowering in itself.

This is the time to commit to the next chapter. So it is time to centre, to breath to get in touch with your inner self and seek out what is important for you for next year. These might be new things, they might be ongoing things or they may be things that you didn't achieve this year but are ready to tackle fresh next year. At this stage it is not about planning them out or doing them. It is about identifying what they are, perhaps listing key points and becoming familiar with how you feel about each one of them.

It is well worth having things on the list that make you feel warm and excited alongside one or two things that will stretch you or that you feel uncomfortable about but you know are important to your well-being or even your life purpose.

It is important to be clear about the things that are necessary and the things that you are just doing out of duty. For the things that you feel are your duty; check whether this really is the case or whether you are just being a martyr? Is there a way of letting go or easing the "duty". Deep down we all want to be the hero of our own life. However, if this is through something that you feel duty bound to do and holds no real love or motivation for you continuing with it, it is unlikely to serve you or the others involved. It actually usually means that something really needs to change. This kind of change flags up the need for careful unpacking of what is going on and compassion for all involved. It is unlikely to happen overnight and it is unwise to make a snap change. However, by identifying the changes needed, you can start to look and feel where things really sit for you and whether this is something that needs to shift rather than staying on the to do list.

When you have your list that you are truly ready to commit to, even if that is a commitment the circumstances around an item on that list needs to change, write it up in a way that you can keep and check on through the year. Feel into each item and speak out your commitment to yourself, to your guides, to a confidant (if you wish) or even a tree! As you speak to them, feel the emotion. If it does not ring true, check what the emotion is that needs to shift to make that commitment real. If the emotion doesn't shift then it might be a commitment you are not ready to make – so move it to your "B" list.

This is a great way of getting the energy up to commit to the things you want or need in your life and being clear about them. It is also a great way of being truly honest with yourself about what you can or cannot commit to. Often we spend too much time doing what we think we should be doing rather than committing to what really makes us grow to enable one to manifest a joyous, loving and abundant life.

The list that you truly commit to place it in a book or box that you can keep in a safe place. You may even want to put a crystal with it, to help energise the list and your commitment.

The tree that connects most with this time, is Birch. This white tree of the forest is all about renewal, new beginnings and is no stranger to the cold and the dark. Its bark has been used for cleansing and writing on for a long time and its sap is very nutritious.

The First Stirrings of Spring

This is the very start of February (in the northern hemisphere). It is that time when winter is still present but there are just the very first signs of early flowers and buds. There is just the slight softening in the air and, if you pause, you can just sense that ever so slight stirring within the earth.

In the Christian calendar it is known as 'Candlemass' and in the Celtic Fire Festivals it is 'Imbolc'.

The invitation at this time of year is to become aware of the light within. The light within ourselves, the light that is returning to earth, the light that is held within each plant and seed that is part of the earth and is getting ready to begin the growth cycle. It is about the seed within and the light within that seed.

This time of year can be particularly taxing as we are nearing the end of the winter cycle and it can be a time when we feel particularly drained or depleted. The outlook can seem particularly bleak.

- **Physical** – We are still in a time where our bodies need nurturing with good wholesome foods and at times longer rest. While there is a sense that it's a new year and we need to crack on actually in many ways our bodies are still attuned to nature, which is saying that the renewal time is not over yet. We are still in semi-hibernation. However, it is a great time to start to get just that little more active. Now is a good time to start to introduce a more regular regime of exercise or walking into your schedule. If you have a garden, now is a good time to start to compost and prep your tools and get ready for seeding.

For those that do really suffer from any seasonal affected disorders, do support your bodies physically with nutrients and minerals and even purchase a day light lamp as these are most effective. It is also about focussing on the things that make us feel good. In any season there are many dynamics; winter is not just cold, dark and wet, it can also be bright and sunny and crisp. It can bring a peace and calm that is hard to find in the rest of year. It gives you the perfect excuse to snuggle up or tackle any of those indoor chores or hobbies that have been pushed to the side during the more outward bound times of the year.

- **Practical** – This is a time of preparation. It is time to make ready for the busy and more external time ahead. It is a great time to start to look ahead what needs to be cleaned out, booked or scheduled in, whether that is building works or holidays or short courses or new health regimes.

- **Emotional and Spiritual** – As mentioned earlier the gesture of this time is about the early stirrings and the light within, within everything. The days are still darker and wintery almost half slumbering. It is a great time for dreaming.

At some point in the first week of February, make some time for yourself to create or be in your own safe and sacred space.

This time it would be great to adorn any space with early spring flowers or shoots, alongside any candles. Allow yourself to centre and be still and see if you can become conscious of that very early stirring of light and life that is all around us at this time, in the skies, in nature and deep within the earth. Become aware of your own inner light and allow these outer and inner light energies to consciously connect and nurture each other.

When you are ready, open up your Commitment list that you made from New Year and see how it looks and feels to you now. Take each item on the list in turn, feel into the emotion you have for it and visualise what it might be like for you; where you might be, who you might be with, what kind of clothes you might be wearing the kind of things that might be around you as you do them. Feel into the emotion of it. Be honest with yourself about what warms you, what creates butterflies and what you do not like.

A key part of understanding our genuine motivation around things that we have committed to is to really, visualise them into being. Allow the images to get as big and as real as you can and allow your motivation and the love for it to grow. Butterflies are actually healthy and I'll come back to these more in the next stage. Where there is fear or resistance but overall you are still committed to undertaking these things allow the inner light to shine brightly and disperse this fear or illuminate what you might need to overcome the fear or a genuine barrier.

When you are ready take some deep and cleansing breaths and be very aware of your body, the ground or chair that you are set on and the physical space that you are in. Allow yourself to make any notes on your commitment lists which include comments about what you love about it, your motivation for doing it, and your emotional hook into overcoming any doubts or fears. This process is just as relevant for those things on your commitment list that are on-going as well as anything you are seeking to start or develop. It is a powerful way of continuing to motivate and develop what you are already involved with.

The tree of this time is Willow. Willow has deep roots and loves water and in many ways is a fantastic water filter. It was for many years the tree that held up our banks and river ways. It is the Dreamer's tree and teaches us flexibility and resilience.

Spring Equinox – the Fullness of Spring

In the Northern Hemisphere this is regarded as the first day of Spring. As outlined in the introduction much of this way of connecting and working is with the natural rhythms of nature, seasons and your body. One of the best ways of deepening our connection is by bringing nature into your daily life. This can be as little or as much as your current life style will withstand. In the spring it is the natural time to plant and seed so the invitation at this point in the year is to start seeding something (even if it is a single pot plant) that can grow with your through the season. If you are not successful or inexperienced, that's ok, just give it another go. Experience is the best teacher.

At the spring equinox we once again find ourselves connected with the time of the year which is perfectly balanced between night and day. This time we are in the knowledge that each day is going to get that little bit longer. For some of us this is just the energy boost we have been waiting for and the mood lifter which propels us into action. For others spring can sometimes feel stressful as everything is getting busy again and our bodies are still adjusting to the longer days and the more active lifestyle.

The gesture of this time of year is about Honesty, Planning, Planting and Nurturing.

- **Physical** – It is not for nothing that this time of year is associated with spring cleans and detoxes. There is nothing better to raise the chi or energy of the house or your body than a good clear out. However, there are often more back problems and domestic injuries during this spring time due to the sudden activities in gardens, DIY and new exercise regimes. So the message is – do, do it because it is healthy, just do it in a way that is mindful to your own capabilities and pace yourself.

It is at this point in the year where the Yin Kidney Chi recedes and the Yang Liver Chi becomes the dominant chi for the growth part of the seasons. I am not going to go into body detoxes in this book as there are many, many sources of information about this. To get you started some good references are "The Five Elements Wellness Plan" by Barbara Temelie, and "Staying Healthy with the Season" Elson M. Haas, M.D.

Furthermore I recommend that body detoxes, especially if you are suffering from any medical conditions, really need to be undertaken with the guidance of a medical or nutritional professional.

- **Practical** – this is the time to really put your plans into action. You many need to make some action plans or schedules for how and when you are going to undertake things in the coming months. However, this is the season for really taking action.

Begin by mapping out what and when you are going to undertake key activities, projects or how to schedule in improved exercise regimes. It is a great time to actually make the bookings for whatever you need for them or purchase the materials and tools that you need to undertake them. If you are facing exams or completion of a qualification then this needs careful scheduling. Make sure that you have enough time for study as well as your other life needs and demands which also needs to include some leisure time.

Get outside as much as you can. If you can plan your leisure activities to include some outdoor activity this will really help raise your energy levels. Conscious connection with nature is one of the most stress relieving things we can do.

As we get busy at this time of year and the diary fills up with activities, it is good to note that nature, although bursting forth also grows at a steady rate and it is good for us to sometimes slow to this.

- **Emotional and Spiritual** – The spirit of this time is the spring rising. The energy is rising and everything is springing into life. This rising energy is also about fuelling fertility and creativity. The gesture of the season is action, clearing out, planning and planting what is going be nurtured and grow through the expansive part of the year. It is a time to get energised and this can happen so easily when tuning into nature.

The direction that is associated with the Spring Equinox is the East; it brings the elements of Air and Wood within the Celtic and Chinese systems. They are about intellect, growth, and planning. With it, hand in hand comes honesty. Honesty regarding what is being sought, the intent and respect to genuine capability. Sometimes as things get busy, we can get stressed; spring time can be a time when some people feel more irritable, this is usually a sign that something is not aligning for them and is blocked.

The invitation at this point in the year is to make time to go on a meditative walk even if this is simply the local park or a favourite open space near you. Get out in nature and connect with the rising energy. You may need to wrap up as it can still be quite cold and muddy. Connect with the nature or trees around you and really feel into their energy. You may become aware of their rising energy and the life that is just beginning to show, or even hasn't quite emerged. If you start to feel too heady, then ground yourself by walking mindfully through the nature or find a tree and connect with its root system below. Most trees have root systems that go as far below as the trunk and branches are above you, this is certainly the case for trees such as the oak or ash. Become aware that things take their time to grow and emerge, so if there are things that are not moving swiftly enough for you in your own life, or things that you are frustrated with, become very aware of this slower and less instant pace and yet the incredible power of energy that is rising.

Allow yourself to revel in the joy of this awakening and make time to regularly connect with nature in this way over the coming months.

Another symbol that is associated with this time of the year and is very powerful is the egg. Eggs are, of course, associated with fertility and birth, they are also protective, nutritious and they all have their own incubation period. You may wish to meditate on this and, particularly if you are feeling vulnerable, stressed or anxious about things that are coming up, to actually feel yourself in a protective egg. Allow yourself to be nurtured and relaxed in this space.

You may also wish to visualise some of the things that you might be working on or trying to develop within your life as being inside an egg, especially if they are still at the stage of being planned and you are at the very start of their manifestation. You may even wish to consider what needs to be in the egg with them to help them grow and be nurtured, just as an egg provides vital nutrient to the unborn chick. Visualisation of this kind can also show if you simply have too many eggs! Are you taking on too much? Have you got the capacity to nurture them properly? Some might need to go into "cold storage" or have longer incubation periods i.e. more than a year, others might be needing some outside help and might be about developing a community or network around them. This is the time to plan and for action so allow these pointers of clarity to come into your consciousness.

The tree energy associated with this time is the Alder and the Ash. The former is about balancing the male and female aspects, while the ash is sometimes known as the world tree, it is about the inner and outer realms. Both teach resilience and a kind of soft power as well as recognising the need to balance the seen and the unseen, the tangible with the intangible. Through the balancing and joining of these two aspects comes a steady nurturing growth and manifestation.

Summer Launch – Start of May

This occurs at the start of May in the Northern Hemisphere and in the Celtic or Druidic tradition is known as Beltane. This is when the spring rising turns into the explosion of summer. Everything is coming alive, budding and flowering; the countryside is teaming with life reawakened and is full of vitality. Everything has that fresh green, freshly scrubbed, ever so new look to it. The bank holidays are associated with labour day, country fairs, folk dancing and music and are all about celebrating, giving thanks and putting energy into the forth coming months of brightness, fertility and activity to bring growth, prosperity and a good harvest.

- **Physical** – This point in the year it is all about getting out and about. If you're a gardener of any kind you will already know this. It is also a time for our diets to lighten and this can happen quite naturally as the weather becomes warmer. Less warm dinners, roasts, hot pots and casseroles and more fresh fruits, salads and yoghurt and other such lighter foods. This is actually a great time to start or press on with a new health regime.

- **Practical** – This is the time of getting out and getting on with things. For all those things that you have been meaning to do or are planning to do, this is the time to put them into action. The days are getting lighter and warmer and we can generally feel our energy levels rise with this change and expansive time of the year. It is also traditionally the time of year for exams and for completing academic projects; it is a time for focus and to push ahead to actually achieve what you want to.

As this is the time to really put into action what you desire in your life, this might include revealing these to others and communicating about your plans, or activities or goals. This is a great way to get the support that you may need. This can sometimes be challenging as it makes it very real and equally you may have to face people who are not supportive or even disagree with what you are attempting in your life. These people are actually great testers of your resolve and often can help us really hone in on what it is that we are doing. If you find it becomes too much of a sabotaging energy, put your energy into finding groups and avenues that will support you and shift your focus away from those who are simply blocking your growth. This will help you to focus practically on what is needed rather than making excuses for not having accomplished what you need to.

- **Emotional and Spiritual** – this can be a very exciting and joyous time of year, when you really are able to forge ahead with plans and activities which you enjoy as well as revel in the uplifting energy of the year. Allow yourself to make time to do just this.

It can also be a little bit scary as one reveals and communicates activities and desires. It really is a time of being brave and moving from thinking and dreaming about something to manifesting it. The energy of this time of year is a fantastic creative energy with the emphasis on creativity. Make time to connect with this creative energy and what it means for you.

This time of year invites you to go out and observe and undertake meditative walks or meditations in nature. Allow yourself to become one with it; you may find yourself drawn to a certain place or tree. Allow yourself to start to visit it on a regular basis and when there allow daily life to sink away through the ground and access your own creativity. See what creative medium might call to you, art, poetry, writing or even something far more tactile like making or baking. This is an invitation to get in touch with different mediums of material and expression that you might not normally use in your everyday life. If you need to do a short course, do it! Most of all, simply bring your joy to it and allow your inner creativity to flow through. This is not about being tested and it is up to you who you share it with. This outlet can help you in many ways in your normal everyday life. Often as we express ourselves in a creative form, even if it is something we fancy but are not very good at. We can find a new way of letting go, exploring, expressing and we can learn a lot about ourselves. A child learns a lot from play; this learning does not stop in adulthood.

If you are feeling at all depleted or overwhelmed, meditating under a tree is a great way to de-stress. Allow the softness of the season to enter into your being. Nature herself as she springs back into life, and forges ahead with a great energy, does it steadily. It is strong but not forced, it is steady but not fast. Allow this to be your anchor if you feel at all pushed or overwhelmed as you forge ahead with your own activities.

The tree that is most associated with this time of year is the Hawthorn. Its medicinal properties help circulation and heart, its expression embraces the 3 phases of the feminine – maiden, mother and crone. Beltane is all about the maiden energy. It is a great tree to connect with, the vibrant, open and pure loving energy of this time of year and this tree is all this as well as being very grounding, aiding balance.

The Apex of Summer – Midsummer Day

The Summer Solistice is of course the apex of the summer light, the longest day, the expression of the fullness of the year. Everything still feels fresh and green and has not ripened yet, and it is in full bloom. It is the maxim (the full 'Yang') of the year. Wherever you are, or whoever you are it is time to come out of your shell, cave or egg – even if it is just for the one day of the Solstice. Both the Celtic and Chinese systems identify the height of summer with Fire. It is the yang, hearty, joyous and outward expression of love, service and celebration.

- **Physical** – At this point of the year it is essential to make sure you stay well hydrated and make the most of all the fresh foods and lighter eating and lighter nights to absorb as much vibrant energy as possible. If you feel ungrounded or over stimulated at this time of year, then being out in nature and especially by the sea-side is incredibly grounding, balancing and relaxing. The combination of fast urban living and summer vibrancy can for some become over stimulating.

- **Practical** – This is a great time to really be 'walking your talk' to the maximum. Whatever this means for you. It might be developing a home business, spiritual practice or health regime; the energy at this time of year will support you. It is also important to plan in some down time especially if you are the kind of person who finds it hard to be "out-there" all the time. Also if you have key events, exams, fairs or competitions, something you have had to build up to deliver, make sure you plan in some celebration and time to regenerate afterwards.

The great thing with the longer days and everything being so alive at this time is that it does not take long for us to replenish. If you find you are the kind of person to get ungrounded or over stimulated, make sure you plan some time in nature or on retreat to replenish in an internal way.

- **Emotional and Spiritual** – Summer time can be a very emotional time of year, lots going on, parties and social events. As a result, while it is good for us to express ourselves and get out and about, it also means sometimes emotions can run high. It is worth being aware of this and allowing space for these things to cool off. In July we have the moon phase called the Thunder Moon; this is aptly named and of course it can be the season for thundery weather.

Amazingly with all this fire and light, it is also the apex, which means that it is the point where the water element begins to rise again as the sun and fire element has reached its climax.

A beautiful exercise at this time of year to centre, energise and balance, involves tuning into this beautiful dynamic. This can be done in your personal safe space or in a sacred place in nature that may call to you around solstice time. Again, don't forget that Solstice means sun standing, so moving with the energy at this point in the year invites us to do the same. Stand still.

Become aware of all the light around you and in every part of nature and become aware of the light in you. Enjoy the feeling of this element being at its fullness – even if the day is grey or wet – remember the daylight hours are much longer. Allow everything that you are involved with at this time to be energised with this beautiful, renewable and ever present fire energy, to be warmed and grow to their apex. If they are things that no longer serve you or you have finished visualise them being gently burnt off by the fullness of the sun and transmuted. Then become aware of the blue sky above you and the rising energy of water. You might even be by the sea or a river, or perhaps even take a drink of water. Allow the blue and the water to cool you, replenish you and wash away any concerns or anxieties you may have. Tune in to how much water is actually around you all the time in the atmosphere, in our bodies and in nature. It is the life giver. The alchemy between light and water is the very essence of life. Allow this to balance and energise you and fill your being. Feel this beautiful soft, yet powerful, solarised alignment between heaven and earth, let it energise and still you.

The flower that is most associated with this time is the rose, which totally vibrates with the same vibration as the heart and the vibration of love. The tree energy that is most dominant at this time is the Oak. He wears the crown of the forest and teaches endurance, together with the dangers of being overly ridged. The Oak is also a home to many species and, as such, teaches us much about eco-systems, how we create our own eco-system and how we are very much a part of the global eco-system and cosmos.

The First Harvest

The energy of this time of year is all about ripening and bringing home the harvest. This is something that, in our modern life, we seem to want to do, or are pushed to do more and more swiftly. Nature shows us and teaches us again and again that, while things can develop swiftly or evolve suddenly, great change can literally occur overnight. If we want something that nurtures us, and provides a sound basis for us either physically, emotionally or even spiritually, it usually takes longer to grow and longer to achieve. Furthermore, everything has its own optimum season or setting to come into full bloom and fruit. This is the same for everything that we do. The more we force things, the more we simply store up problems for ourselves and sometimes others too. This does not mean we give up or do nothing, what it does mean is that we listen to ourselves and to whatever it is that we are engaged in. We don't bully and force but we listen and find the most healing and constructive way to achieve what will support and nurture us, others and the environment. In many ways, when we find what works with the environment, the other two fall into place as we are part of this greater, older (and frankly wiser) system.

Traditionally this time is known as 'Lammas' or 'Lunasagh' and was celebrated at the start of August. It is when the white summer sun becomes the golden sun, everything ripens and the corn is harvested. It is about starting to gather in, just as within the harvest the seed for the next year's crops is contained, evaluating where you are and what is going on for you. When we are clear on this, the channels for re-dreaming where you are going are opened up. This time of year has a dreamy quality to it and the energy supports you in this.

Traditionally it was also the time to get married. There is a lovely story in the history books that suggest William Shakespeare and Anne Hathaway were brought together at this time of year for the local harvesting and fell in love. In the Autumn, they were officially married and then very soon their first child was born.

- **Physical** – This is a time for really allowing yourself to revel in the summer and summer fruits. This does not mean giving up work or stopping whatever it is that you are doing, but it does mean allowing yourself to make the most of this nurturing and very earthy and warming energy. It is a great time to top up Vitamin D (through being outside) as well as all the summer fruits which are plentyful at this time of year. If you enjoy gardening, now is the time that you can enjoy the fruits of your labours (or it's a great time to get freebies from friends or neighbours who do and might have a sudden glut of fresh produce). If you can bottle and preserve, then this is your time to start stocking up for the winter months. Just think of all that sunshine you are bottling for those darker months!

- **Practical** – This is also the traditional time for holidays, so make the most of the break and top up. It is also the time to celebrate, particularly if there are people in your family or life who have passed exams or are preparing to embark on a new chapter in their lives for example going to study at University or new job after graduation of some kind. While bringing the harvest home might take a bit of effort, it is also time to make time to lean back and enjoy – this is the time for making hay so you can remember those hazy summer days. (the other jobs can wait for a bit!)

- **Emotional and Spiritual** – As already mentioned the gesture of this part of the year is about gathering and bringing in the harvest. It is a great time to evaluate where you are. It is also a great time to revisit some of your commitments and dreams and even re-dream where it's appropriate.

This time is the start of the inward journey, while still physically being very much a part of the outward expression. So the invitation is to get out in nature as much as possible to make the most of the warmer season. Make some time to go for meditative walks, find a place where you feel safe or return to a place that you love and allow yourself to connect with the trees and space about you. Allow yourself to tune into this incredible golden time of the year and the ripening and harvesting process. Allow yourself to also be aware that this season lasts for several weeks as everything ripens at different times and some right into the Autumn period. Allow yourself to really take stock of your own life and where you are, what you are doing and what the key themes of the year have been and still are for you. How are these supporting you or helping you to grow? This growth is about personal development and health just as much as it is about any financial matters. In fact in many ways more so as without the personal well-being it is difficult to make any changes to your financial status.

This is your time to reflect and connect with your own inner path, as opposed to concentrating only on the practical money and bill paying cycle. This is your chance to take stock at a deeper level, enabling you to make room or check that room has been made for these deeper needs.

Where advances have been made, allow yourself to grow with them and enjoy what has unfolded. Allow this to be held and warmed by the energy of the ripening late summer. Give thanks. Become aware of what the next steps might be, the seeds that are within, and what is now on the horizon for the next stage or chapter. Just become aware of these.

When you are ready, consider the things that have not come to fruition or have "failed". Allow the abundant energy of this time of year to show you what you have actually learnt and achieved and what still holds you attached to these issues or times. Gently harvest your golden seeds of wisdom from this. For those things that no longer serve and have no place in your life, allow yourself to say good bye and let the summer sun burn the links off or the summer rains wash them away. Allow the energy of the season to become the new energy within you rather than the ties to things that do not serve. If it's something that you are sad to see the end of or release, give yourself permission to mourn it or shed a tear if need be. In releasing this energy you are making space for the new. This is not about blame, hate or anger.

If these emotions are there, own your part of them, and release them constructively. Walking, writing and forgiveness practices are key to shifting this kind of energy.

Depending on what is going on in your life you may need to do this exercise a few times through the summer period. However, it is an excellent time to release, harvest and receive your seeds of wisdom so that you are energised and have some clarity on what it is you seek in your life as the year begins its descent into the darker days.

There is a dreamy almost romantic quality too to this season, the hazey summer days and the soft summer rains, travels and trips away. So it is an excellent time to be still; allow yourself to connect with your inner light and dream new things or realign your dreams about what it is you want or need. The practical 'how' can come later when you revisit your harvest and the balance in your life at the Autumn Equinox.

The tree energy that is dominant at this time of year is hazel. It is known as the tree of wisdom as it is the divining wood and enables insight to come within, even if the rational mind struggles to make sense of it. For eons, hazel wood, which is flexible and strong and directs energy very cleanly and quickly, was (and still is) the wood that gets used the most for wands, dousing, walking staffs, and for weaving structures such as shelters, arches and gates.

This brings Part I of this book to a close as the cycle continues and moves to Autumn Equinox. Contained here is an overview of the seasons, their associations and gestures. A practical guide as to their meaning, energy and how you can engage with them on a physical, practical and sensory level. The invitation now is to use this guide and to deepen your exploration each time, making it relevant to your needs and life. There are many avenues that you may find beneficial to explore even deeper, such as the dietary and produce of the season and the medicinal properties of the plants and produce, enabling you to undertake the practical actions in a conscious and mindful way.

You can make the meditations and connections as ceremonial as you wish or bring in some of your own existing spiritual practice. This will add focus and energy and likely increase what you will receive from them. The tree and elemental references provide very rich and insightful dynamics and there are many good books and references which can help you understand more. However, often one of the best ways is to simply be open to the experience and finding your own outlet or expression. Just remember the fundamental rule – be grateful, be respectful and to quote the age old wiccan saying –

"Do what ye will, harm none, do none harm!"

Over the seasons and the years as you use this guide and explore areas deeper, the experience will change. Every year is different, so although you might think you are just doing the same thing over and over again, there will be a different emphasis. You will no doubt find yourself in different places or drawn to different aspects, which will be the most important for you at the time.

Part II will take you through the Chakra system and it's associations with the energy body. It is important in anything where we are seeking to develop a great connection, understanding or clarity, that we first begin by understanding ourselves. From here we can begin to see and go on to actually experience that life does not just happen to us but we are co-creators of our world.

Part II is a great personal development resource in itself, and it contains a programme of how this can be related to the seasonal cycle to aid personal balance and empowerment. This brings another dynamic to energise you through the year.

PART II

Chapter 4
Understanding Your Chakras

"Dare to love yourself as if you were a rainbow with gold at both ends."
Aberjhani, Journey through the Power of the Rainbow: Quotations from "A Life Made Out of Poetry"

The chakra system is now widely known in the western world, although its roots are from the eastern practices, primarily Yoga. It is an energy system that interestingly echoes key nerve and gland centres within the body the broad principles of which have been recognised across many different healing systems and cultures. Although the symbolism and associations may vary between the different systems, there are incredible similarities between them. Given that all of these systems developed in different cultures, terrains and independently across the world, they have stood the test of time. This would strongly suggest that, however we wish to describe it, there a flow of energy through the body which contains key nodal points or energy centres. Each of these energy centres has particular characteristics and functions. They essentially connect the physical self to the ethereal and emotional bodies.

You may ask what has this got to do with working with the seasons, seasonal connection and having quality time. Working with the Chakra System allows us to access and be in touch with our inner well-being and balance, it can help one to ground, centre and to receive insights. The different associations and gestures allow us to gain better insight into our own ability to push, pull and create within our lives. Combining the knowledge of this system with the Seasonal connection and fluctuations can provide a profound and powerful way of moving forward for a life filled with quality, insight and colour.

Part II works with the main Seven Chakra system, and then combines this system with how you may use it in the seasonal work. As with Part I, it contains practical exercises. It is important to note that there are a number of other chakras which exist in more extensive energy body systems which these are not covered in this book.

Root Chakra

One of the best ways of becoming familiar and tuned into the Chakra system, your Chakra system, is by sitting still, closing your eyes and taking some deep breaths. Just focus on the breath for a while. You can use a count of 4 or 6 for the in and out breath, to slow and even each breath. When you feel more centred and focused, take your attention into your body, feel into the chakra areas and visualising the colours of these chakras as shown in the illustrated image and outlined below. As you do so, be aware of what you feel in your body, or the emotions that come to the surface or see in your mind's eye as you connect with these different areas and chakras. The 'Root chakra' is at the base of the spine and pelvic floor area. The 'Sacral Chakra' is mid-point between base and naval. The 'Solar Plexus Chakra' is at the base of the rib cage and diaphragm. The 'Heart Chakra' is in the heart area, the 'Throat Chakra' is at the base of the neck and the throat area. If you feel more up in your jaw or mouth area, this is just energy associated with this area, it is not the chakra itself. 'Third Eye Chakra' is in the middle of the forehead, above and between the eyes. 'The Crown Chakra' is, just as it suggests, just above the head connecting with the top, like a crown. Feel into these areas individually to locate them in your body. This should be done each time before beginning and after any more focussed or intensive work on one or more particular chakra(s).

This helps to ensure that you connecting with the energy system as a whole and ensures better balance in the long-term.

Chakra 1 – The Red Root Chakra

This chakra is positioned at the base of your spine and forms your root.

- <u>**Sanskrit Name**</u> - Muladhara - Root

- **Associations** – tribal, physical, survival. Gesture, I am. Element Earth. Colour Red.

- **Role of the Red Root Chakra in our lives** - this chakra is most dominant in the first seven years of our life. It is all about the physical nurturing of our boundaries as well as feeling or being safe and that our basic survival needs are being met. It gives us our roots, and our tribal ties and often is about the culture within which we grew up, which is often the source of our basic belief systems.

Nurturing and Understanding your own Root Chakra.

This Chakra is all about our roots, our physical life, our family and/or tribe, blood links and is key for being grounded. Without being grounded or having healthy roots just like trees we become unbalanced and are liable to topple.

The positive energy is power and the negative is fear. Therefore, to move forward in life, a healthy root chakra is essential. Makes us able to face and overcome the challenges of life. This is about facing and overcoming fear where it has no place. It helps us to know the difference between the "good butterflies" and the "anxiety butterflies". This is not about just over riding the anxiety or ignoring our fears as sometimes "fear is wisdom in the face of danger, it's nothing to be ashamed of." (Sherlock in the Abominable Bride).

To support the root chakra and your whole being it is key to undertake regular grounding techniques. Often we get too wrapped up in our daily tasks. It is always good to practice them during any meditation or any transcendental or any other altered state practice. Grounding techniques include:

− Walking in nature

− Being consciously aware of the ground beneath you and your feet on the ground.

− Being consciously aware of the breath in your body.

− Eating something nutritious and staying well hydrated.

− Doing simple tasks mindfully. Gardening, cleaning or cooking for example.

− Being around or working with animals.

− Wearing or having things around you which are red, even eating red foods.

Caroline Myss works through the Chakras in beautiful and incredible depth in her book "Why People Don't Heal and How They Can". In this work each Chakra has a key expression and healing affirmation. For the Root Chakra it is; "I connect to all that is in my life. I am filled with energy of gratitude, and I am allowing that energy to flow with all its strength through my physical and spiritual body".

You can use this affirmation in meditation focusing on your root chakra.

The chant sound for the root chakra is UM or LAM chanted as low as possible. (Reference "Chakra Frequencies" by Jonathan Goldman and Andi Goldman). Chanting these will help to vibrate and clear and energise the root chakra enabling it to be balanced.

Crystals which support the Root Chakra are: Hematite, Garnet, Jasper, Obsidian and Apache Tear. Include some plain quartz when working with these crystals to help clear and lighten any heavy energy in this chakra. The energies held in this chakra are often connected to areas in your life which are associated to this chakra. The Root Chakra associations include: your family, your "roots", community, physical concerns of safety, ability to know and hold safe and nurturing boundaries, and your past even your past life associations. Place the crystals on or near the chakra or meditate with them.

To look deeper into gathering your power, releasing fears and strengthening this Chakra or just for support it is good to consider:

- Who is your tribe? These are the people you are born into, your family and your nearest companions and closest friends. Who are they?

- Who do you attract into your life? What kind of people generally?

- Who would you like to attract into your life and why?

- Before making any decisions to stay, change or move out of your existing "tribe" it is worth checking why you you've reached that decision. What is it they bring to your life and what do you bring to them?

Sometimes we can find that there is a mis-match between who is in our life, the kind of people who are coming into it and the kind of people we would like to help and those we'd simply like to be with us, given where we feel we would like to be. Frankly the people we have in our life is far more a reflection of ourselves than the people themselves. So if you would like better friends (whatever that means to you), or nicer clients, or a more supportive network, first you have to be and secondly you need to look closely at what you are doing and where you are generally "hanging out", which includes mentally and emotionally not just physically. There is another dynamic which is about authenticity. If we find we are living a life that is making us miserable or trying to be something that we simply are not, the chances are we are not being honest with ourselves and are very far from being authentic.

As we make the internal shifts so our external world changes, but remember we are walking a spiral, so the healthiest shifts happen gradually. Allow them to evolve with you and you to evolve with them. This allows for a more grounded approach and we can be kinder to ourselves and those around us. As we all learn the lessons that we need to, it enables us to move on, rather than to run-away. Running usually results in the same process simply starts again just in a different place with different people.

Working in this way we are also less likely to become closed off and become a victim of our circumstance. There's a good story to remember about the dangers of doing this and it is the story of the Frog. If you tried to place a frog in hot water they would leap out, if you place it in cool water and gently heat it, they don't notice and eventually die. So by being more aware of what you are choosing to be a part of, you are less likely to become the seduced frog!

Chakra 2 – The Orange Sacral Chakra

- **Sanskrit Name** – Svadhisthana - Sweetness

- **Associations** – relationships, fertility, sexuality and creativity. Gesture: 'I feel'. Element: Water, Colour: Orange.

- **Role of the Orange Chakra in our lives** – this chakra is most dominant and forms within the second 7 years of our lives, aged 7 – 14. It is about our relationships not just with our parents and our immediate family but also our friends and the ability to form long lasting, close and nurturing relationships with others and our "significant other" whoever they may be. It is the seat of our creativity and power to manifest.

Nurturing and Understanding your own Orange Sacral Chakra.

The Sacral Chakra is all about creativity and close relationships, fertility and birthing or even rebirthing.

The healthy emotional energy for this chakra is creativity. When blocked or out of balance the key emotional energy is Guilt. The Bach flower remedy Pine is very good for this as is being with the tree itself. The Sacral Chakra is, an incredibly important part of our body, for what we create in our lives as well as being the seat of our power. It is, this area that gets invaded if abuse occurs. The energy effects on someone's life can be very profound. Such energy powers what an individual will go on to do and their ability to create in their lives and how they are able to nurture close relationships.

In Tai chi and Qigong it is this area that forms the heart of the 'Dan Tien', an area of power and grounding that is nurtured and balanced within these forms of exercise and practice. The 'Sitting Horse' or '3 Circles' is a very helpful stance for grounding and centering to build the energy in this area. A good reference is "Everyday Qigong Practice" by Richard Bertschinger.

Simple breath work, breathing to the count of 4 (four in and four out), while focusing on this area and sitting or lying down is incredibly stabilising and calming.

Focusing on the gaps between the 'out breath' or the 'in breath' are, in many ways, gateways to other attention states or the 'turning point' i.e. key for release and renewal. Combining concentration on this area while noting the gaps between breaths can help to access what is held in this area; typically either energy blocks or release for creative flow. This helps you to gain insight into your own creativity and where it is held, as well as nurturing your instinct about issues or situations. This relationship is especially strong in women due to the presence or space for the womb.

It is good in meditation to place your hands on this area and just sense in and ask what is held there. Invite the colour orange in to surround and energise this area, show what is there, clear away what is not needed and to heal. Consciously breath into this area each day.

The healing affirmation for this chakra is; "I am a vessel of creation. I am magnetically alive and I am able to create life". (Reference: Caroline Myss.)

The Chant for this chakra is OOO or VAM "see "Chakra Frequencies" by Jonathan Goldman and Andi Goldman for more details.

Crystals which are supportive for this Chakra are: Carnelian, Unakite, sunstone, rhodachrosite, moonstone, orange opal, Jasper, Chrysocolla, amber. Place them on or near the Chakra or meditate with them.

Wearing orange or eating orange fruits or meditating with the colour orange can help to revitalise this area.

This chakra is also associated with the element of water so activities which involve water, being by the sea, swimming or spa baths (i.e. bath taken with epsom salts and natural oils) are very healing.

Use all of these techniques and tools to help you to centre and connect with your authentic, creative self. If you know of, or uncover, deep trauma, use the tools to help you observe, move and transmute the energy to light or nothingness (whatever is held in this area). If you feel it is too much then seek appropriate advice and help. However, these practices will help your progress while undertaking any other therapies or counselling programmes.

Once the creative juices do flow another dynamic often opens up allowing us to move into the creative zone, which can be a totally blissful state. We need to be aware that sometimes there is a need for us to become a little bit obsessive in many ways about our subject or whatever it is we are creating which may also require some form of discipline. We do, however, need to become aware of when we are becoming obsessively stuck. At this point we need to put it down for a while and do something else, some form of physical exercise, engaging in "normal life" and trusting in the beautiful creative energy that goes on creating. When we return, we can often be surprised to find that we have progressed and are able to use fresh eyes and fresh views to add to it's vibrancy rather than ploughing on in the same way.

Chakra 3 – The Yellow Solar Plexus Chakra

- **Sanskrit Name** – Manipura – lustrous gem

- **Associations** – Solar plexus, in the mid of the abdomen, Personal Power. Gesture, 'I do'. Colour Yellow, Element Fire.

- **Role of the Yellow Chakra in our lives** - personal power and ability to stand our ground, and make our way in the world. It is particularly dominant and forms during the third 7 years (14 – 21) of our lives. It is about forming wider relationships, including with our peers, taking our stand in the world and making our way. It can also be associated with the Ego. In balance though it is simply our presence and our ability to take our stand.

Nurturing and Understanding your own Yellow, Solar Plexus Chakra.

This Chakra is all about personal power/will-power. It is about the ability to take our place in the world and be potentially expansive. It is the colour of yellow, of the sunshine, bringing in light.

Emotional energy when in balance is about will-power, when injured it is about shame. Ego can also play a big part in how this energy plays out in our lives. While it is about taking a stand it is just as much about how we take that stand. In balance it enables us to do so in a loving and an authentic way rather than via a stiff or controlling manner. In balance this energy comes from a centred and playful place; when pressured it is our sensor for stress or nervousness or our anger. If you feel depleted or attacked, placing your hand(s) over this area and breathing into it will help rebalance and will avoid being dragged into an emotional state that is not helpful for you or for others.

The healing affirmation is; "I am filled with the energy of endurance and honour. My thoughts and words carry the power of creation itself." (Caroline Myss).

The chant for this Chakra is OM or RAM. (see "Chakra Frequencies" by Johnathan Goldman and Andi Goldman.)

Detoxing can help this area to clear.

Yellow colours are energising while browns help to ground and find boundaries if things have got out of balance.

Supportive crystals are: Citrene, amber, tiger's eye, sunstone, orange opal and orange carnelian. Place on or near the Chakra or meditate with the crystals.

A good meditation is achieved by steadying the breath, filling into this central area and feeling our etheric energy body for it's shape and boundaries, strengthening them where needed and unhooking any chords or connections which do not feel light or are draining us. When unhooking etheric energy chords, just visualise removing or cutting them and sending them with love and light back to where they came from. Allow the light and breath to clear away any anger or heaviness.

Chakra 4 – The Green Heart Chakra

- **Sanskrit Name** – Anahata - Unstruck

- **Associations** – heart space, the seat of the soul, love, compassion. Gesture, 'I love'. Colours: Green and/or Pink. Element: Air.

- **Role of the Green Chakra in our lives** – Some systems describe this as the seat of the soul, other systems say the seat of the soul is the liver or the third eye. Though slightly confusing, there are good reasons for these differences and they all hold an energetic truth. In energy terms, the heart is the central meeting place of the intellectual and higher consciousness of the mind and spirit and the physical and instinctive knowledge of the body. It is definitely the seat of love and it the best place to check-in with when trying to make a decision which goes beyond and is more subtle than simply right or wrong, or yes or no. It is the place where we find truth, our passion, our purpose and our calling. This chakra is most dominant and forms during the 4th phase (ages 21 – 28) of our lives. Interestingly, this is the time most of us are finding our way in the world in terms of careers, partners and starting our own families.

Nurturing and Understanding your own Green Heart Chakra.

The Heart is of course the centre of love, kindness and compassion and guides us in finding and manifesting our purpose in our life.

The colours are green and pink and the emotional energy swings between Love and Grief.

The healing affirmation is; "I ask the Divine to fill my body and spirit with the healing power of love strong enough that I can feel it's power. I need this power so that I may heal and live a full life". (Caroline Myss).

The chants for the Heart Chakra are AH and YAM (See "Chakra Frequencies" by Johnathan Goldman and Andi Goldman).

Supportive crystals are aventurine, rose quartz, ruby, malachite, beryl, bloodstone, emerald, moonstone. Place the crystals on or near the chakra or meditate with them.

Healing plants for the heart are roses, which vibrate at the same vibration as the heart energy. Placing just a drop of pure Rose Essential Oil on the heart chakra can ease it. Mugwort essence can be helpful to clear grief and resolve difficult relationships.

A great meditation for the heart space is to again focus on the breath and on the heart chakra, allowing it to be filled with pink or green light. Allow this loving energy to fill your heart and flow to someone you love, even if there have been difficulties. Just allow this eternal energy to flow to you and through you.

Chakra 5 – The Blue Throat Chakra

- **Sanskrit Name** – Vishudha - Purification

- **Associations** – Throat, speech, truth, song, taking a stand, responsibilities, thyroid. Gesture: 'I speak'. Element Aether or Spirit

- **Role of the Blue Chakra in our lives** – It is the centre of communication so we can sing out our message and our truth to the world. Through this can come a great deal of creativity. It is closely linked with neck and shoulders and the ability to reach out. The throat chakra is dominant and developed during the 5th phase of life (ages 28 – 35). This is a time in our lives when we are well on our path and need to take a stand or stand our ground and speak our truth to the world and to our families.

Nurturing and Understanding your own Blue Throat Chakra.

The throat Chakra is all about speaking our truth, taking a stand, personal expression, communication. It enables us to open up, to have rapport with the world around us and enable us to have an authentic expression. Its lessons are all about correct communication. It is just as much about knowing when to be silent as it is about making a noise.

The emotional energy of this chakra is truth and lies.

The healing affirmation for this Chakra is; "I hold you in gratitude, and I withdraw every circuit of my energy from all that I have judged". (Caroline Myss).

This affirmation holds key messages of gratitude and removes judgement that we may hold about others. If we are to communicate well and truthfully we have to start from a place of gratitude, kindness, compassion and love. If we hold judgements or resentments, then it is these that will be heard and held in the communication and in our own energy bodies until it is dealt with, resolved or transmuted to light or nothingness. This affirmation helps us to move out of a place of being blocked or angry so that communication can flow again, which, in the long term, can be healing.

The colour blue is supportive for this chakra and is of course, used a lot in marketing for anything that involves communication, since it flows like water.

To enable clear speech and remembering that this chakra is also linked to our shoulders, it is important to check in on our responsibilities. Make sure we are in balance with what they are; are there responsibilities we are not facing or are there ones we've taken on which are not ours? This can happen at a subliminal level and it's healthy to check in on this on a regular basis. If we are not clear about these things in ourselves then we cannot clearly communicate them to others or resolve or deal with them. This just adds to pressures, stresses and miscommunication.

Activities which are great to free up this chakra are singing, poetry or prose, and chanting. Chants for the throat are "EYE" and "HAM" ("Chakra Frequencies" Johnathan Goldman and Andi Goldman). Chanting, singing and prose can really help this area open and align as this Chakra is the voice. Chants or singing also require good breathing and help to bring into the body a vibration that lifts the chi and help unblock not just this chakra but the body as a whole.

Crystals supportive for this chakra are; turquoise, kyanite, lace agate, sodalite, calcite (blue), lapis lazuli, blue tiger's eye. Place on or near the chakra or meditate with them.

A good meditation is to bring in the blue rays and the Azure ray which are very protective and connect with the Divine. This can help clear and protect this chakra and your whole energy body.

Chakra 6 – The Indigo or Purple Third Eye Chakra

- **Sanskrit Name** Ajna - Perception

- **Associations** – Third eye, pituitary and pineal glands, insight, psychic abilities. Gesture: 'I see'. Element: light/dark

- **Role of the Purple Chakra in our lives** – This chakra is about giving us both insight and foresight. The clearer and more balanced this is the more we can weigh things up or see different aspects and perspectives to things, situations and people. It is very mental and is the seat of intuition and so is therefore closely associated with psychic, clairvoyance and higher consciousness. It is also know as the seat of the divine soul and is associated with the connection to our divine and higher self; the part that never incarnates in the physical world. It is developed during the 6th Phase of life between the ages of 36 – 45, and is about our enlightening, our vision, and our ability to see ourselves and beyond the superfluous, bringing in challenges of clearing away emotional debris or clutter and exercising forgiveness in all things in our lives.

Nurturing and Understanding your own Purple and Third Eye Chakra.

This is the Chakra of insight and the visionary, the psychic and is often associated with access to bliss during meditation or heightened states.

The energy of this Chakra is Insight and Illusion. It invites us to see things compassionately, releasing blame and judgement and to connect with the Divine. In this process we are likely to have to open to our shadow side; the side of us whch for most of the time, we are subconscious to, it is what lies behind our habits, emotional out bursts, and judgemental belief systems. Call on Archangel Zadkiel to help you release blame and judgements and to for work through any issues of forgiveness. You may be surprised what starts to turn up in your life or what you feel drawn to do, by waking with the purple chakra.

The healing affirmation is; "I release the limitations of human reasoning toward others and towards myself. I live in trust and I have no more questions". (Carolyn Myss).

The gesture of this affirmation is about shifting out of the "yes but" brain, into the inner calm, mindful, holding the intension and energy of release and trust.

Chants for this chakra are "EYE" or "SHAM" ("Chakra Frequencies" (Johnathan Goldman and Andi Goldman).

Supportive colours are violet, mauve, purple or indigo.

Supportive crystals are; Amethyst, charoite, Lapis Lazuli, pietersite (which is great for grounding the etheric body), Covelite. Place these crystals either on or near the Chakra or meditate with the crystals.

Suitable meditations are those that include good grounding techniques, combined with the opening of the third eye. This can be done through breath, using the chants and focusing on the third eye. It is important to note that such practices are likely to bring up stored emotions and should not be pushed. Regular practice helps to clear blocked energy. However, pushing for results just causes stress and could be more detrimental than helpful.

Mindfulness practice and positive affirmations are very helpful for clearing away negative or unhelpful thought forms which block an individual and the third eye. Clearing away negative thought patterns can shift our view of the world and those around us, making our lives flow better. Working on this chakra can bring up negative emotions, stored memories or areas where we harbour anger. By remembering them we can release them and forgive ourselves and those involved.

Dadi Janki in her beautiful book "Wings of Soul" writes how we can only forgive when we remember, when we remember, we need to ask ourselves what it is that is holding us in this moment. When we find that answer and can let it go, forgive it, then we are free. We might never forget what has happened but we can forgive it and we can be emotionally free from it. From my own experience, it is also fair to say that just because we forgive someone for their actions, does not mean we have to let them back in our lives, or allow them to treat us in the same way. If we do and the energy has not shifted to one of better care, than we are simply leaving ourselves open to the same treatment. Forgiveness is not about being a doormat. It is about releasing the pain, hurt, anger or resentment to the situation or the person or ourselves. It is about learning from what happened but not in a bitter way that closes us off to future experiences, but in a way that actually prepares us for how to handle similar situations better. It enables us to be more able to recognise the dynamics of situations, including people's own hurts as well as our own folly, so we can be wiser and more compassionate next time.

Certain foods and chemicals are particularly damaging for the third eye – too much tinned fish for example, salmon, tuna or chemicals such as fluoride, are some of the worst. This area is governed by the Pituitary gland which is not only associated with psychic development, but has a very important physical function such as sleep patterns, through the balanced production of melatonin.

Through regular meditation, chanting and detoxing, a balanced third eye chakra can enable inner peace or "bliss" and better sleep and clarity for making informed and insightful decisions.

Chakra 7 – The White Violet and Crown Chakra

- **Sanskrit Name –** Sahasrara – Thousand Fold

- **Associations** - Connection to the divine, to the beyond, and bliss. Gesture: 'I understand'. Element: space and Etheric

- **Role of the White Chakra in our lives** – The White Chakra is just above our heads, and is about the energy that brings in thoughts and thought manifestation. It enables transformation and transcendence. When it is open and balanced it helps us to see the bigger picture and evoke trust and faith, enabling us to receive and connect with inspiration. This Chakra is particularly dominant and comes into its own in the seventh phase of life, (ages 46-52). It is about seeing the bigger picture and connection to the divine; having the capacity to rise above things, to reach for higher ideals and manifest something greater in one's lives and in life in general.

Nurturing and Understanding your own White Crown Chakra.

The essence of this chakra is all about self-love, loving acts and beauty, and connection with the Divine.

When in balance it is about connection to the divine or cosmos; when out of balance the challenge is about attachment and ego. It is the chakra that can become most easily blocked or out of alignment.

The healing affirmation is: "I have no focus, I have no question, I empty myself of all weight and worries, I am union" (Caroline Myss).

This is about letting go, having faith, trust and being held by the universe. When people block this level of connection, it often results in depression, and judgemental or bitter behaviour.

Thankfully, this chakra responds easily to music, chanting and the environment and, by being in places or atmospheres which resound with a higher vibration, this chakra can come back into alignment. It is all about beauty and seeing the beauty within. The first step back to grace is through gratitude; being grateful for what you have right in front of you.

The chant for this chakra is "EEE" or "OM" ("Chakra Frequencies" by Johnathan Goldman and Andi Goldman.)

Crystals which are great for aligning this chakra are: quartz, amber, amethyst, celestite, selenite. Place on or near the chakra or meditate with the crystals.

Activation of this chakra is particularly receptive to detoxes or fasts. It is important, though, to undertake fasts in the right way and choose one that suits your body, as well as preparing beforehand and coming off fasts gently so as not to shock your system.

***

As you work with the Chakra system, you are likely to find that there are times that one or more particular chakra(s) need more attention or deeper work given the associations and issues that are associated with each chakra. Use the tools, affirmations and chants to enable this work. However, be aware to always check into all the chakras before and after any of this more intensive work to aid balance and grounding.

Chapter 5
Powering up! Working with the Chakras and the Seasons

All the exercises, chants and tips on supporting each chakra are great to work with at any time. It is also important when working with one chakra in particular to have regard for all of them and to tune into each one in turn, so that they remain in balance. Chakra work can be done at any time of the year and can form part of your own regular meditative practice.

However, working specifically with each at a certain time of the year or tuning in specifically with one or more in line with the gesture of the season can be incredibly profound. It can provide depth and insight to the seasonal work as well as clear or add an important energy dimension to the process.

This section will take you through which chakra(s) to work with at the key seasonal gateways and provide guidance on how to work with them in line with the seasonal gesture.

Mandala of the Seasons

Seasonal Celebration and Chakra Exercises

It's great to work and strengthen the Base or Root Chakra at the time of the Equinox. The Spring Equinox is at a time of the year where the energy is rising and we are entering a very active time. To make the most of this powerful energy, good grounding is needed as well as a sound base to work from. The Autumn

Equinox is the reverse, the energy is turning sharply inwards and is about retreating, reviewing, gathering in. To realign with this shift, a sound base is important. It is also a very earthy time of year, so it is a great time to strengthen this energy as it is easy to access and tune into. At Equinox the energy is all about balance, without a balanced base chakra or strong roots we ourselves cannot be balanced.

Alongside the Equinox Exercises outlined in Part I of this book, the invitation is to spend some time tuning into the Base Chakra and all of its associations and to use the supportive tools and activities outlined previously.

The Equinox as (both Spring and Autumn) are preparing you for the next phase of the year, either the inward winter period or the more external and active summer period. In preparation it is important to know what and who are supportive for you for the next six months. So make a list considering the following:

- Who is your tribe (this can be family, friends or colleagues)?
- Who is the kind of person you attract?
- Who would you like in your life?
- Who do you need in your life to support you? What do they bring to you and what do you bring to them?
- What makes you feel supported?
- What helps you to feel centred and safe?

- Make a list of 10 practical steps to support you in achieving your dreams for the next six months.

Summer Launch and Gathering in for Winter

These times are about creativity and fertility. The Summer Launch is about manifesting your dreams and plans, finally taking them out into the world and being active and creative. During the Gathering in for Winter, getting in touch with the sacral chakra helps us to access our intangible and inner creativity and instincts through the inward journey, reviewing and releasing anything that is finished or no longer serves us. The Sacral Chakra is our creative centre it is important to ensure that it is clear, unblocked, balanced and well nurtured.

Shift in diets are likely to be occurring at these times either to a lighter summer diet or to one which is more warming and nurturing. Diet helps to keep this chakra unblocked, balanced and supported. By consciously meditating and connecting with this chakra at these times it is easier to understand these changes better as well as any emotional shifts that might be occurring. When there is better understanding and acceptance of something, often it no longer controls us and it can either be released or a different approach can be taken. Listening is one of the most simple and yet profound ways healing can occur.

Meditation to get in touch with this chakra at these creative and releasing times of the year is of great benefit. Again, use all of the techniques and materials already outlined for these times of the year as well as for the sacral chakra, as you feel it calls to you.

A special meditation you may wish to do is to meditate with a theme of colour orange, using crystals and pumpkins as appropriate at this time of year.

Settle yourself and centre yourself. Place your right hand on your heart and your left hand on your lower belly, on the sacral chakra, and allow the breath to ebb and flow between these two key chakra points. With each breath just invite it to go a little lower until you feel a comfortable but relaxed breathing rhythm that moves between your chest area and your lower abdomen. Become aware of how these two areas are linked. Take your attention to the sacral chakra, and tune into what it is that you are creating or wishing to create in your life. As your breath moves allow what comes to the surface to be "sense checked" by your heart. For those things that make your heart heavy, check in if they are things that you actually want to continue to create in your life. If not, it is time to let them go. Allow things which make your heart sing and have a lightness to grow in front of you, in your mind's eye. These are the things for you to focus on. If you have a dream that your heart is yearning to create but you have been blocked, now is your chance to sense what those blocks are.

Through your sacral chakra, check what it is that is blocking you. Some blocks may at this point just fall away as you realise they are nothing to be feared, or you already have the skills and resources to move past them. If they are genuine issues with which you require more help, identify up to three things you can do (even if this requires help from others or a course or new skill'), identify what they are so you can start to genuinely remove these blocks from you own divine creativity.

As you can feel the way forward opening up, sense it again with your heart and what sits in your heart. Bring an Orange light into your sacral and pink and green into your heart chakra to energise them and empower you to manifest your creative choices. Allow those things that need to be let go to fall away down into the earth where they are composted and transmuted by her own red and orange fiery energy.

Solstice

The solstices are key apexes in the year and are about standing still, absorbing, celebrating, taking stock, and aligning for the new cycle. They are both about power, either external and expressed or one that is about to be reborn; they are about passion and they are about the divine connection to the cosmos. So, at these two apex times, it is great to tune into the Solar Plexus, the Heart and the Crown Chakras. Each chakra also connects with each of the three soul cauldrons: the Physical Soul, the Etheric Soul and the Higher Self Soul (that never incarnates).

This exercise is about bringing you into alignment with that part of your being which is about the physical and manifest, with the inner you and with your higher self. Solstices are powerful times of the year, and they really invite us to pause, for that is what the sun is doing, and to align and realign.

The energy will help you do this, and it will also show you that which is not in alignment for you.

This exercise can be done sitting or standing, best of all standing out in a place of nature. Allow yourself to really straighten and feel yourself connecting with the earth below and the sky above. Become very aware of the solstice energy and the gesture of the solstice, be it the summer, at the apex of expansion or winter at full contraction for rebirthing. Allow yourself to become filled with the energy of the earth beneath you and sky above, the fullness or the renewing of the sun energy. Feel into your abdomen area and allow each breath to build this energy within you. Become aware of your own energy and energy body, how it feels, how big it is. Let it be aligned and energised by the renewing energy of this time. In the summer this might feel very expansive, which is great to bask in. In the winter, it might feel more subdued, but allow it to become very solid within you. The energy is still; it can be very steady and incredibly powerful for letting go and renewing. Both Soltices are very potent times to let go of the ego will and realign with your authentic and heart centred will.

When you are ready, feel into your heart. Allow your heart to be filled with the solar energy of this time; allow your heart to speak to you, revealing what it holds most dear. Allow any hurts to be either burnt away by the fullness of the summer sun, or let them fall to the ground and be taken deep down into the earth where they are composted and transmuted just as the energy goes deep within the earth through the winter time for renewal. Allow your heart to expand and connect lovingly with all that is good around you. Listen very carefully to what sits at the centre of your heart and connect with your own heart's calling and purpose.

Then move to your head area and your crown chakra, become aware of the sky and star energy above you. Allow yourself to energetically grow upward and connect with this ever bright and ever renewing energy. Allow this to become a column of light that comes down all around you, aligning you fully between earth and sky. Feel the power, steadiness and love that is held within this strong connection. Let this feeling and this light sink deep within you, so you can recall it at any time.

For the coming months call on the memory of this strong and connected feeling to help you energise and enlighten your intensions for anything that you are either in the middle of doing and dealing with in your life, or that you have finished with and are seeking to release or that you are wishing to reconnect with.

First Harvest and First Stirrings

These times of years are all about preparing. One is about getting ready to gather in, to see the reality of ones labours, while the other is about getting ready for the way ahead. They both require insight and clarity. They are both about self-expression and often require clarity of communication. The Chakra that are great to work with at this time are the Throat and the Third Eye.

At these times and to work with these chakras, it is particularly beneficial to do regular chanting or singing or drumming practices to clear the throat chakra and the energetic lines of communication. Taking salt and oil baths would be very helpful as well as using oils such as lavender or frankincense.

Both of these times of the year have almost a watery depth to them. First Harvest is the time of the water element starting to rise; first spring stirrings is the rising of energy and new life being born from the deep and watery depths of the earth. So it is about going deeper and allowing things to flow from within.

At these times, spend some time feeling into your own inner wisdom and insight and determine what needs to be expressed and how you might wish to do this. Don't forget that expression is not just about words, it can be written, or described in pictures through some other art form. Allowing yourself to connect with different mediums will give you insight into what you really want to say and help you to connect to your own expression. Often when we allow these more creative channels to open, it can help build confidence and improve our more ordinary daily communication.

PART III

Chapter 6
Integrating these Practices into Everyday Life and Situations.

Hopefully you have now gained a good insight into the very powerful rhythms and gestures that the seasons hold, which are going on around us each day and every year. As you work with them, develop the connection practices and use the techniques and guidelines in this book and even go on to refine your own way of working with them. You will come to see how they actually contain the gestures and stages of any process that we go through in life. This is true whether it's about a life stage, relationship, project or developing a skill, hobby or job. They all pass through to some degree or other a stage of:

– Inception

– Motivation

– Planning

– Activation

– Fullness

– Harvesting

– Taking Stock

- Finishing

- Releasing

- Remembering and Renewal.

However, some things we deal with in life do not match the annual calendar. While the recommendation and invitation in this book is to use the seasons and their very clear rhythms to help you re-centre and gain clarity and insight aspects of your life for your own overall well-being, some things won't wait for 'the right' seasonal celebration. This chapter is about how you can use what is contained in this book in a flexible way to help you gain the insights you need for remaining in balance and making clear decisions and remaining focussed.

The first step is understanding where you are in the cycle. Is the issue that you are dealing with is it at the point of inception, planning, requiring action, or the nurturing stage? Is it in need of releasing or aknowledging an ending point? What are your emotions about it? It is important to understand whether they are emotions of enthusiasm, joy, or anxiety, shame, or even grief. Sometimes there might be a mixture, but, by becoming clear on what you are feeling and why, we can often find the answers to what needs to come next. You can do this by meditating and sensing into your chakras.

Find the season or seasonal expression that is most relevant to the issue that you are dealing with, it's stage and your emotions around it. While it does not necessarily match the year's cycle in months, the issues are still subject to the same kind of cycle. Use the techniques in the relevant season cycle phase to help you gain better understanding about the issue and the emotions that are associated with it. For example if it is something that is just at inception and you need to get motivated, use the techniques and qualities that you would use for a celebration at First Stirrings of Spring, combining these with the Chakra exercises.

If it is something that you are needing to activate and get behind, then use the base and sacral chakra exercises together with the equinox and spring launch expression. If you are feeling anxious, know that you need to do more work on your lower chakras and personal power to build this up.

If you are at a point of full expression and still feeling anxious, check in with your heart centre. Is this actually something that you believe in? Perhaps you heart is no-longer in it. When we have little passion for something our power rarely follows and you may find that you are trying to force something that isn't going to come. Until you find the joy in it, you will be struggling. Find the nectar and everything will start to move for you. Use the Solstice Exercises.

If you are dealing with an ending, or failure and a release then turn to the seasons which are associated with this, the Winter Gathering and the Winter Solstice. It may be time for a compassionate clear out. Be gentle on yourself and other involved.

It is worth checking in on how you generally feel about stages of the process itself. Some of us enjoy beginning things, some of love being "out there", some hate clearing up or can't bear endings, while others love the tidy up and good closure. Understand how you relate to these things generally and you may well find that the answer to some of your difficulties lie simply in your own relationship with these aspects. Use the relevant Chakra Exercises and seasonal practices to strengthen your relationship with these weaker areas and seek the joy in them.

Chapter 7
Facing and Healing Difficult Anniversaries and Annual Celebrations

"In every ending comes a new beginning. Sometimes they overlap; Sometimes there seems just space between. It's there because we need to be still or we need to heal."

Tanya Adams

So far the programme of exercises, meditations and techniques in this book have been very much about connecting and understanding the stages and power that is stored in each season to help us grow and shift in an ever changing world. They provide a deeper understanding and connection between ourselves and the natural rhythms are both around and within us every day; we are not separate but are very much a part of the environment and the world we live in. This is even the case in our modern society that likes to insulate us from the rigors of nature. These rhythms go deep and help us steer through the changing landscape of our days, our own seasons and phases and our lives. Hopefully, you will already be practicing many of the techniques and enjoying this deeper connection and gaining your own insights into what these mean for you and how they play out for you in your daily life.

However, what has not been described in detail so far are those anniversaries or seasonal celebrations that hold painful or difficult memories. These are not just restricted to the death of a loved one. There are other difficult anniversaries, for example, the end of a relationship, an accident or ill health that changed lives profoundly. The failure of a business, loss of a job, or failed qualification are other difficult anniversaries. The death of a loved one of course is something that will never be forgotten and, while the pain does ease with time, this point of profound change never ever really goes away.

Observing mindfulness, being present in the 'now', letting go, together with forgiveness exercises all help to ease the pain of these things and help to move on. However, there is often a point where we are reminded of them so acutely so that we cannot escape the sinking feeling, sadness or even anxiety or stress that they bring up.

It is worth giving yourself some time either at the anniversary or, if you have other things that you know you're going to have to do or face actually on that day, making some-time before hand, so that you can listen to yourself, and give yourself some space to allow the emotions to be released and to build up your strength to face whatever it is you need to face.

If it is a difficult or painful memory, set some time aside so that you can connect with the memories that arise and that need to be witnessed and held. If you allow yourself to do this in a space where you feel you are safe, undisturbed and nurtured, it can provide an important emotional release. You may want to write some of them down, or express them through drawing or music. Allow yourself this time with these memories.

If anger or frustration results, a non-destructive way of releasing the energy can be through going for a walk, writing or punching a pillow. Allow it to emerge and diffuse. Allow the pain to be replaced with forgiveness of yourself and/or the other party, visualisation of using purple crystals or light colours or saying you forgive them are all very powerful ways of shifting this energy. Even write a diary letter. That is a letter that you don't send but simply write symbolically to the person. If you wish you can dispose of the letter afterwards as a way of releasing the emotional energy.

If you are feeling loss and separation, know that you can always send them love whoever and where-ever they may be. Allow the space created to become new space in your life; fill it with light and focus on the things you do have and those which you want in your life, as the space is now there for you to let these good things in.

Using the techniques and practices contained in the Autumn and Gathering in Season Sections are very good for this, as well as those in The First Stirrings of Spring.

If you are facing an activity or challenge that is bringing up memories of failure, or that you feel you can't face because of previous bad experiences, or perhaps simply it is pushing you beyond your normal "safety zone", spend some time just reflecting on those previous times and consider all the things that are different about now compared to then. This might lead to increased self-knowledge, additional skills and perhaps better support that you may have now. Spend some time meditating and working with the Red to Yellow Chakras or rather Base to Solar Plexus Chakras, work to build up your roots and personal light power. In addition, work with the Throat Chakra, to help you open up your communication channels and enable you to speak your truth. If you are still feeling anxious, check in with the heart chakra and see if this is really something that you are passionate about. When we find the love in what we are doing, or about to do, the vibration lifts since love has the highest of all emotional vibrations and will help to realign the emotional perspective.

The spring and summer rituals are great for this type of emotions and confidence building. You can still connect with this vibrancy, even in the depths of winter through visualisation and music.

Finally there may be times when you simply need to withdraw from an activity or an anniversary gathering and give yourself time to recover and to hear the inner you. Give yourself permission to do so. Sometimes there is a fear that if we do this, we won't ever go back and "face the party" and so it is easy to get pushed into a mind-set that says carry on whatever. If we don't give ourselves the space to hear and heal the pain within, then it will find another way of expressing itself. Sometimes this can become the most destructive of all, manifesting itself in many ways within us including aggression and illness to name just two. Don't forget life is a spiral and we may and do re-join "the party" when we are ready; it just might be a different "party" to the one we were a part of before. However, if we are brave and do the work, it will be a party that we choose to join with rather than attending out of a sense of oppressed duty. This is a very important part of living a life that is both empowering and authentic.

About the Author

Tanya Adams founder of Pathwayfinder, a Shamanic Reiki Practitioner who is trained in traditional shamanic healing techniques, geomancy and space clearing as well as being a Reiki Master (including Reiki Drumming), Crystal Therapist and Bach Flower Remedy Practitioner. She works with the Chinese 5 Elements, Taoist philosophies, Feng Shui, as well as the Celtic 4 Elements and Tree Medicine.

Tanya grew up in the south-west of England, and as a young woman pursued a professional career in Urban and Transport Development in London and undertook a number of travels around the world, before being called to her Shamanic path. She has built up a depth of knowledge and experience of embracing the challenges and wonders of walking between the worlds of spirit, nature and 21st Century living.

Tanya is passionate about living in harmony with nature and its rhythms. She says; "I believe that both the physical as well as the emotional and non-physical need to be supported and work in harmony for a healthy happy life. I feel my previous academic and work background gives me a down to earth and analytical approach where needed. However, my own experience has been that healing has more usually occurred not by analysis but rather through compassionate tracking of the non-physical, emotions, and energy blockages and by releasing and expressing these in a safe environment and in a focused way. Nature has an incredible way of enabling, teaching and holding this kind of deep and transformative process. Personally it has led to a better level of understanding and a re-connection with mind, body and soul, which had previously been injured. All of this enables an overall better sense of well-being.

www.pathwayfinder.wordpress.com

Made in the USA
Middletown, DE
12 November 2017